"I have spoken to and counseled with hundreds of Christians, especially pastors and former pastors, who are trying to find God in the dark days of their faith journey. When it seems as though nobody understands, Dave Shive is a welcome comfort who can truly say, 'I know how you feel.' He has been there. Recognizing the pressures, frustrations, and disillusionment of God's apparent absence, *Night Shift* not only offers one man's story but every Christian's hope."

Dr. Gene Getz
Senior Pastor, Fellowship Bible Church North
Director, Center for Church Renewal

"Finally, some help for all who are stuck on life's night shift. Dave Shive writes from experience; he's been there and done that. You'll not only relive the dark hours of life with him, but you'll rejoice in the insight he brings to all who are living in those same dark hours right now. There's light at the end of the tunnel—and it's not an oncoming train. It's the bright hope that God can use us mightily after we've learned the lessons of the night shift. This book will encourage your family, friends, and you. It's biblical, practical, helpful, and readable."

Dr. Woodrow Kroll
President and Senior Bible Teacher
Back to the Bible International

"I first met Dave Shive in 1989 on the eve of his 'night shift' experience. This book resulted from that time and is a serious look at the hard side of life and ministry. With striking transparency, Shive pulls back the curtain on the window of his own soul to show us one man's search for God and his finding answers to meet his need.

"The reality is that the discouragement and seeming abandonment of the night shift experience is being repeated in men and women today, and far too many are so surprised and shaken that they give up hope.

"Wherever you are on your spiritual pilgrimage—at the beginning, or the end, or maybe stuck somewhere in the middle—this

1

book will remind you that God is near, very near . . . even during the darkest hour."

John Fletcher
Former President and Current Director of
National Ministries, PIONEERS

"Dave Shive and I have been friends for thirty years. He was one of my first spiritual mentors and deeply influenced my life and future ministry through his enthusiastic Bible teaching, passionate basketball coaching, and godly personal example of a loving husband and father.

"My friend Dave has lived and toiled on the 'night shift' and has learned some powerful lessons about what God is doing in the dark. I am grateful to God that with this insightful book, we can all understand more of the mysterious way that God works in our lives."

Pastor Dave Epstein
Senior Pastor
Calvary Baptist Church, New York, New York

"All of us have faced difficult periods in our lives. We know by experience that God 'hasn't promised us a rose garden.' At the same time, it is important that we learn to react to negative circumstances in a Christ-centered way, because such a reaction turns bitterness into joy and sorrow into gladness. Dave Shive has been through all this personally, and in a wonderfully readable style, he shares with us the despair and the joy through which God brought him. I highly recommend this book as a practical approach to Jobian issues."

Homer Heater Jr.
President
Washington Bible College and Capital Bible Seminary

NIGHT SHIFT

God Works in the
Dark Hours of Life

DAVID A. SHIVE

Mark - Our God is so wise!
He redeems our adversity for
our good and His glory!

Dave
Ps. 119:71

BACK TO THE BIBLE
Publishing

NIGHT SHIFT: God Works in the Dark Hours of Life

BACK TO THE BIBLE PUBLISHING
P. O. Box 82808
Lincoln, Nebraska 68501

Editor: Anne Severance
Assistant editors: Rachel Derowitsch, Allen Bean
Cover design: Laura Poe
Interior design: Robert Greuter & Associates
Art and editorial direction: Kim Johnson
Author portrait: William Banks

Additional copies of this book are available from Back to the
Bible Publishing. You may order by calling **1-800-759-2425** or
through our Web site at www.resources.backtothebible.org.

1 2 3 4 5 6 7 8 9 10 – 05 04 03 02 01

ISBN: 0-8474-5533-5

Printed in USA

For Kathy
quintessential mother, grandmother, and wife

Your children rise up and call you blessed.
Your grandchildren will say that you excel them all.
Your husband says your worth is far above jewels.
The Vineyard Owner calls you "good and faithful servant."

ACKNOWLEDGMENTS

For an author, no man is an island, and I can assure you that a small army of individuals has made this volume possible. Although I cannot properly thank everyone who has contributed, I must at least express my gratitude to some.

Tom Bisset, president of Peter and John Ministries in Baltimore, sojourned with me on my thirty-month night shift assignment. Always at my side or across the breakfast table, my faithful friend guided me through that formative experience. I doubt that this book would have come to fruition without his support.

Marcia Hornok of Salt Lake City was my first editor before I knew what an editor was or how desperately I needed one. She graciously invested countless hours in the preliminary manuscript ideas and sustained my morale sufficiently to enable me to persevere through the manuscript's infancy.

The early technical assistance of Dr. Homer Heater, president of the Washington Bible College and Capital Bible Seminary, was invaluable. Indeed, his gracious permission to pursue this venture was critical.

Thank you to the members and former members of First Baptist Church of Hereford, Community Bible Fellowship, and Stillmeadow Evangelical Free Church. These communities of the committed provided the laboratory for this inexperienced "scientist" to explore and develop the principles contained herein. For tolerating my foibles and blunders, I am immensely grateful.

Finally, thank you to Back to the Bible for its unbelievable assistance provided in so many forms. Vice President Tom Schindler's initial support was essential for the final stages of the project to proceed. Matt Poe's expert publishing know-how and encouragement to a babe-in-the-woods was welcome. The reader will recognize the expert eye of Laura Poe in the graphic design of the book. Kim Johnson wisely and capably directed the production of the book from beginning to end.

Last, but not least, my undying gratitude to my editor at Back to the Bible, Anne Severance. It was she who took the meandering pen of a would-be author and helped me produce a book that I could enjoy reading. Thank you, Anne!

TABLE OF CONTENTS

FOREWORD

Every two months or so, Dave Shive and I meet for breakfast in a restaurant on Baltimore's west side. I delight in these breakfasts. The food, coffee, and service are excellent, and the retro fifties ambiance fits us both perfectly.

Normally, this combination should be enough to explain why we have kept this tradition alive for so long. Just a couple of friends with common interests enjoying some time together over orange juice, scrambled eggs, bacon, fried potatoes, and whole wheat bread.

But this is not the whole story. Something else is happening at this breakfast. It's called Christian fellowship. It's two guys, clearly past their prime on the racquetball and basketball courts, experiencing the oneness of mind and spirit that only followers of Jesus Christ can understand.

The amazing thing is that there is never enough time. Dave is bright, aware, educated, and thoroughly evangelical. At the same time, he's different because he likes to challenge the status quo while always remaining scrupulously true to Scripture. I like the challenge of fresh ideas and different points of view, so Dave's ramblings are invariably interesting to me. We race from subject to subject, covering every imaginable topic: politics, sports, culture, music, theology, missiology, worship, archaeology, elder care—on and on we go until, exhilarated and exhausted, we rise at the established quitting time, shake hands, and promise to do it again.

But there is more, for in these breakfast meetings lies something else that makes them a special treat for me. Dave is the real deal. He practices what he preaches. The Christian faith is alive and well in his life. I was there when he and Kathy went through the difficulties he tells about in this book. I saw him descend into a deep, dark pit and watched him emerge from it a couple of years later a more devoted follower of Christ. Through it all, Dave never became bitter or ungodly in response to his trials. Yes, he agonized over his troubles, and more than once he wondered where God was. But he never doubted God, never turned aside. I can learn something about the Christian life from someone like this.

Night shift? "Been there, done that" is the shortened version of Dave Shive's story. If you want to know whether or not faith in Jesus Christ has anything to offer you during the hard times in life, read Dave's book. You'll like his honesty. And, you'll find his insights helpful, especially if you are struggling with the question of God's purpose in the struggles of life.

Before you read this book, or perhaps before you read each chapter, I encourage you to consider the words of Job in the Bible, chapter 23, verse 10: "But He knows the way I take; when He has tried me, I shall come forth as gold."

Tom Bisset, President
Peter and John Ministries
Baltimore, Maryland
January 2001

I waited intently,
waiting and waiting for Jehovah,
and He turned aside to me
and noticed my cry for help.

He lifted me out of a noisy pit,
from the slimy mud,
and made my feet to stand upon a rock.
He stabilized my steps.

He placed a brand-new song
in my mouth,
a song of praise to our God.
Many shall notice and be afraid
and shall be full of confidence
in Yahweh.

Psalm 40:1–3
author's paraphrase

A PARABLE OF THE
NIGHT SHIFT

S tepping outside into the early morning air at the conclusion of another staff meeting, Michael was energized. Every encounter with the Owner and His Son renewed Michael's enthusiasm for their mutual enterprise.

The awakening sky sharply outlined the green entrance sign with its bold lettering, which read: **Kingdom Vineyard.** Long rows of grapevines extended for as far as the eye could see. Top-quality machinery sat waiting for the crew of the morning shift as its members eagerly assembled at the front gate. Kingdom Vineyard maintained a first-class operation.

It was 7 A.M. As the fatigued night shift workers shuffled through the rear gate, the day shift chatted in small groups near the entrance. Breathing a sigh of relief that the sun was up, Michael, the foreman, clamped the morning employee roster to his clipboard.

The change in mood was dramatic as a fresh crew arrived for the day's work. The air was charged with laughter and conversation. Bubbling with enthusiasm, wives, husbands, pastors, missionaries, and a variety of other laborers came to work in the vineyard.

Michael casually watched as they eagerly pressed through the gate. Most of his challenges would come later in the day.

15

Throughout the morning hours and into the early afternoon, the workers bustled about their work, singing, whistling, laughing, and chatting freely. The machinery always worked properly in the morning, and very few distractions hindered these employees as they plied their trade. Soon the storerooms would overflow with grapes, fine wines, raisins, and jellies—all ready to be delivered to Ethne Market. The workers delighted in their partnership with the Owner as He distributed His wares.

Throughout all of this activity, Michael observed the Owner's Son mingling with the laborers. Smiling broadly, the Son laughed and conversed with all who passed His way.

When the 3 P.M. whistle blew, the afternoon shift was already assembled at the front gate. Pausing momentarily to admire the day's production before heading home, the morning crew knew that its efforts had been crucial to supplying the outlets of Ethne Market with needed products from Kingdom Vineyard.

Paperwork in hand, Michael again headed for the front gate. Disheveled in appearance and somber in mood, the second shift arrived for work with an air of resignation. Michael observed that the vineyard atmosphere was changing noticeably.

The afternoon crew's varied problems made focusing on vineyard production goals a complex challenge. Nevertheless, reports indicated that the yield of this shift always equaled or exceeded the first.

As evening arrived, darkness began to settle in and the work became increasingly difficult. Workers would occasionally collapse under a heavy load, equipment would intermittently malfunction, or a few malcontents from Reptile Farm would come by to stir up trouble. When it was totally dark, all equipment was shut down until morning, and the work was done completely by hand.

The Owner's Son also worked alongside this group, His hands and uniform soon stained. Conversations between these laborers and the Owner's Son were less frequent and more subdued. A few second-shift workers actually complained to Him about their assignment, concluding most conversations with a request for a prompt return to the first shift.

The griping continued until second-shift employees heard the signal of the vineyard horn.

At 11 P.M., it was pitch dark as they headed for the rear gate. Time for the night shift.

In the darkness, the workers had straggled toward the front gates of the vineyard. With a heavy heart, Michael carried the roster for the graveyard shift to the gate. This was the part of the day he dreaded most.

Gripping his clipboard, he checked individuals through. Problems were legion among this group: some were ill, most were poor, a few were elderly, the majority was discouraged, but somehow they always managed to show up at the appointed hour. Many of them were also pastors, missionaries, evangelists, youth workers, or Sunday school teachers. They entered with pained expressions and dragging feet. Some had once enjoyed working the day shift and were now puzzled at what they viewed as a permanent demotion. Now they wondered how long they could function in the dark.

What most of the crew had not noticed upon entering the vineyard courtyard was a weathered sign, partially hidden behind some shrubbery: **WELCOME TO THE LAND OF FORGETFULNESS.**

Michael noted that the Son was active throughout the nighttime hours, but because the work was being done under cover of darkness, very few laborers could see His faint image. Some of them had even been overheard during a break complaining about His absence.

Michael had also noticed the attitude of those who had been moved recently to night duty. Their introduction to the shift had been marked by bitterness and grumbling as they grew to resent the difficulties created by the darkness.

Michael could vividly recall seeing the Owner's Son quietly moving among the laborers. The darkness had disguised Him to all but a few discerning Night School graduate students. Shockingly, the Son's clothes were coated with dirt and His hands were

17

grimy. Sweat streaked His cheeks and dust settled in the lines on His moist face.

Noticing a struggling worker, He stopped to help lift a heavy bucket of grapes. He picked up the branches another had dropped on the ground. Knowing that still another laborer was nearing exhaustion, the Son used a hand to help him place one tired foot in front of the other. Though the workers were oblivious to the Son's involvement, Michael knew how costly the night shift was for both the Owner and His Son.

Barely sixteen hours earlier, the sunny vineyard had echoed with laughter and singing; now the only sounds heard in the murky shadows were groans, sobs, and muffled cries for help. . . .

Deep in thought, Michael headed down the hallway. The door to the Owner's office was ajar, and the sound of voices caught his attention. Apparently management was having a production meeting. Michael paused to listen. The Owner and Mr. Guide, the vineyard's able night school teacher, were reviewing the production reports from Auditing.

"Look at these figures!" Mr. Guide exclaimed. "Why, the vineyard is more productive than ever! Most likely due to the efforts of the night shift."

The Owner smiled as He rocked back in His chair. With constant good news from the vineyard, He relished staff meetings. The personnel office was adding new laborers by the hour. The main storeroom was involved in constant construction, with new wings being built to hold the growing inventory produced by the workers. Many from the vineyard sales staff had even volunteered to undergo extreme hardship in order to saturate Ethne Market with information about vineyard products. Best of all, the market was purchasing more and more of the fruit.

But out in the shadowy vineyard, two night shift laborers struggled to load a large bunch of grapes onto the wagon. Pausing for a moment, the weary men straightened, wiped their brows, and looked around their dismal work area. "This is such a waste of our time and talents!" muttered one to the other, unaware of the Son as He lifted their heavy burden and hoisted it onto His own broad shoulders.

"If I have found favor in Your sight,
let me know Your ways that I may know You,
so that I may find favor in Your sight."
Exodus 33:13

Make me know Your ways, O LORD;
teach me Your paths.
Lead me in Your truth and teach me,
for You are the God of my salvation;
for You I wait all the day.
Psalm 25:4–5

Restore to me the joy of Your salvation
and sustain me with a willing spirit.
Then I will teach transgressors Your ways,
and sinners will be converted to You.
Psalm 51:12–13

Introduction

The Night Shift Principle:
How God Works in Life's Darkest Hours

A blast of wintry rain and wind tore through my uniform. As a driver for a major petroleum distributor in the winter of 1991, I had just completed a heating oil delivery to a Baltimore row house. Braced against the chill, I was rewinding my delivery hose at the back of the truck in the alley behind the house. This particular alley was a gallery full of portraits to human failure; trash, garbage, and junk were strewn everywhere.

I pressed the rewind button, hardly noticing the whine of the electric motor as it labored to retract two hundred feet of heavy hose onto the reel. My thoughts were far from the miserable setting of the alley. I contemplated my home, situated in a rural setting a halfhour from this wretched environment. Though I lived some distance away, I was bearing the sorrow of my own broken dreams—the shattered aspirations of a seminary graduate and veteran pastor.

My mind flooded with reminiscences of sermons preached, Bible studies taught, counseling sessions held, and leadership meetings conducted. My heart was still in the church, but my feet were firmly planted in the debris that bore witness to broken lives—mine and others.

During this winding of the hose, a daily ritual that I performed as often as twenty to thirty times during an eight-hour shift, I happened to glance down. Amid the evidence of societal ruin—smashed furniture, raw garbage, old toys, used syringes, empty beer bottles, and filthy rags—I noticed that I was standing on a used disposable diaper. Recoiling in disgust, I kicked away this blatant reminder that I was out of my element.

That soiled diaper became, at that moment, a pointed message to me, a modern-day equivalent to Saul's spear quivering in the wall next to David's head (1 Sam. 18:11; 19:10). When Samuel anointed David to be the next king of Israel (1 Sam. 16:1–13), David entered a long season of struggle. His goal was often survival, with King Saul in hot pursuit. The spear lodged in the wall next to David's head merely served to remind him that Samuel's prophetic word regarding his kingship was far from realization.

For many readers, a foul diaper may be only a minor annoyance. For me, this innocuous piece of plastic and cotton became a statement of the sullied condition of my life, a poignant reminder of unfulfilled dreams. It accented my deep frustration, varied disappointments, and smoldering anger at the inexplicable dilemma of a vocation apparently gone awry. For reasons known only to God, I was suddenly thrust into the darkness of the night shift.

The multifaceted features of this shift combine to intensify all suffering, even the most miniscule of life's trials. Thus, this fetid household item was very significant to me, for it symbolized my tarnished vocational, financial, and emotional condition.

"My God, My God, Why Have You Forsaken Me?"

Entering vocational ministry in 1972, I was a hesitant, yet compliant, servant of the Lord. I did not glibly agree to serve Him, nor did I select the pastoral ministry as a career. God seemingly picked through a pile of broken people, culled me from the lot, gave me my orders, and sent me forth with a grand vision of churches planted, sermons preached, souls converted, and believers discipled. In that commissioning ceremony, I can recall no warning that there would be suffering, misunderstanding, hurt, betrayal, frustration, or disappointment. And so I went forth in the name of the Lord to serve my God and eventually go to my reward in heaven.

During those first nineteen years of full-time ministry, there were no accusations of misappropriation of funds, immorality, or any of the customary "sins of the trade" that often demand the departure of a pastor from the ministry. Though a fallen sinner like any other, I had been enabled by God's grace to conduct myself with honesty, integrity, and purity.

It had been my lot, however, to struggle with minimal visible results of my efforts. Unlike those pastors whose ministries are marked by healthy numerical growth, wide opportunities to serve, and vibrant congregations, I found myself plagued by seasons of conflict and limited fruit—all this despite the frequent encouragement I received from congregants and friends, assuring me that I was a gifted teacher, able administrator, and competent leader. *If I am so capable,* I would often ponder, *why do I seem to make so little impact on the lives of people? Why does our church struggle so profoundly under my leadership?*

The only answer I could produce was that I had been "mysteriously called" to suffering in ministry. Not having yet mastered the "darkness" passages of the Word of God, I was unaware of the fact that those nineteen years were an appointed night shift season. Much like David, who spent well over a decade as a fugitive from Saul's wrath, I was experiencing a time of ministerial reeducation. Spears vibrating next to one's head and filthy diapers underfoot are the appointed teaching tools in the hand of the Master Teacher.

In addition to the normal trials of pastoral ministry, twice I came under criticism evolving into major personal crises. These were enigmatic periods of great confusion, murky times when each person involved is right and yet all are wrong. Though some of my strategy was successful in fighting those battles, I was young and made the mistakes of youth.

Much like the argument of Paul and Barnabas at the end of Acts 15, fractures do happen between sincere believers. And as with Paul and Barnabas, when the Bible does not take sides in resolving disputes, godly men and women today may also occasionally find themselves stalled in their attempts to find resolution. Such was the case in my problems.

For nineteen years I had studied, prayed, counseled, and sought to use the gifts God had given me for His church. But the work was hard and I frequently deemed the benefits scarcely commensurate with the energy, time, and pain invested. My wife and I agreed in March of that year that it was time to make a change. We were confident that other ministry opportunities would quickly open for us. And, while exciting proposals seemed imminent, all of those doors closed quickly. And so, at age forty-five, when I should have been firmly established, I exchanged my vocational tools of pulpit, books, and people for trucks, oil, gloves, rags, and hoses. . . .

The hose was rewound and I was ready to move on to my next delivery. Pausing for a moment, I leaned against the side of my truck, pushed my cap back on my head, and reflected: *How did a nice seminary graduate like me end up like this?* But deep within, a far more troubling and profound question was beginning to form. My thought took the form of an ancient and agonizing cry that has found its way to the lips of many servants of the Lord: "My God, my God, why have You forsaken me?"

What Happened?

You need not be in full-time vocational ministry to ask similar questions: How did I get to this position in life? What has gone wrong to bring me to this stage? More pointedly, many children of the King may view the disarray or affliction in their small world and wonder what He is doing. Countless godly individuals, trapped in difficult circumstances—"pit" experiences, in the terminology of Psalm 40—have also pondered the course of events that brought them to their current predicament. They, too, are standing in the midst of debris, with a spear vibrating near their heads, and they can't understand why God would allow such a thing to happen.

This book is for Christians who perceive that God has lost track of them in the darkness. Perhaps He is distracted or confused or indifferent to their plight as they bumble about on the night shift. The questions these afflicted saints pose to Him are these:

Will Your wonders be made known in the darkness?
And Your righteousness in the land of forgetfulness?
(Ps. 88:12)

Ah, yes, the land of forgetfulness. Much like a child anticipates presents on Christmas morning, suffering believers, who are faithfully serving the Lord, generally expect blessings. And like children whose Christmas turns out to be a disappointment, God's children may sense that He has forgotten all about them. Puzzled by the contradictions between their hopeful expectations and the reality of their Christian experience, they are in the dark, seemingly forgotten by God. While others press on, they are genuinely mystified by the strange detour their journey has taken.

Rather than giving them beauty, God has placed ashes on their heads. Instead of dancing, their lives are full of mourning (Lam. 5:15). They pray, but their prayers seem to stop at the ceiling. These believers are working in the dark (Ps. 88:6; 143:3).

The Darkness Is a Busy Place

Disciples of the Master, while laboring in some aspect of full-time, part-time, or lay ministry, naturally marvel at the mysterious workings of a God who calls them to toil in His vineyard (often initially against their will) and then seems to abandon them to ravenous wolves. Young wives may be brokenhearted that their dreams for a long and joyous marriage have been shattered by the unfaithfulness or selfishness of their mates. Middle-aged men are frustrated at the inexplicable course their lives have taken: their wives seem unattractive, their children are in rebellion, their finances in disarray, or their careers in disorder. For each of these, and others, God appears to be absent, perhaps weak and ineffective, maybe preoccupied with other matters, or simply disinterested in their circumstances. These individuals are all doing night duty.

To all such laborers, I say, "Press on! Don't give up!" But I must remind all struggling believers of the central proposition of this book: *There remains a season of night shift experiences for every servant of the Lord.* Each believer can depend on the recurrence of seasons of trial and difficulty.

The Word of the Master assures us that these are times God means for good (Gen. 50:20). While we might naturally judge the brightly lit hours as the most important part of the day, not every creature soars in the sunlight like an eagle. Significant things also happen in the nighttime hours. After sunset, dew moistens grasses and flowers. When sunlight fades, nocturnal animals forage and drink at twilight. Bats eat insects and raccoons come to the river at dusk. These creatures sleep through the day when it is hot and dangerous so that their life-sustaining labors can be accomplished at night.

Beneath the surface of the earth, where it is dark and eyes cannot probe, an entire world functions. It is there that coal is made, potatoes grow, worms enrich the soil, ants make their tunnels, and animals raise their young in burrows. In the depths of the ocean, millions of creatures swim and live in the dark, never observed by the human eye. Even insects do their work under rocks. This is God's remarkable design for His creation.

As darkness is essential for vital processes in the physical world, so it is with the spiritual realm. After all, if the signature of God can be found under a mere rock or in a remote creek bed, what great theology can be learned on the night shift in the darkness of the Kingdom Vineyard? Though the dark is a formidable impediment for mere mortals, darkness and light are alike to Him (Ps. 139:12). Nighttime is no obstacle to God; in fact, the dark appears to be an asset that He employs with ease. He is quite comfortable with the night shift and has been known to do some of His best work in the obscurity of shadows.

The stories and principles that follow confirm what every believer finds in the Handbook they read each day: God has worked in the past and continues to work in our circumstances in much the same way He operates in creation—*sometimes in the sunlight but often in the darkness.* Jesus toiled in the darkness for most of His earthly ministry and now commits Himself to the night shift roster so that each member can benefit from His personal supervision and tutelage.

Payday . . . Someday

Beyond the reaches of human imagination, an awesome task has been undertaken. All disciples will be astonished when the final computations are given and the productivity of the afflicted is divulged. This mighty work of our Father will result in a throng of believers who have been conformed to Christ's image and who will bring Him glory throughout eternity. But for now, eye cannot clearly see the astounding activities taking place in the dark.

One day the Father will call an end to all work. Retirement from vineyard labor will occur and each will receive a final paycheck. Every vineyard employee will be stunned by the largesse of the Father.

Special bonuses proportionate to the time spent on the night shift, however, will be dispensed. While all laborers will be presented together to the Bridegroom as a flawless virgin bride, without spot or wrinkle, the night crew will hold a distinctive place in the heart of our Savior, who was called "a man of sorrows" (Isa. 53:3; see also 2 Cor. 1:5; Phil. 3:10; Col. 1:24; 1 Pet. 4:13). Their "bonuses" will properly reflect the exacting demands of those night labors.

The message in Scripture is clear: Suffering has its natural reward. Jesus assured His disciples that their earthly loss in the pursuit of obedience to His call would result in later reward (Matt. 19:29). Paul's writings reflect the lofty value of martyrdom (Phil. 1:18-26 and 2 Tim. 4:5-8), often stressing the rewards and crowns that our Lord intends to bestow on believers (1 Cor. 3:14 and 2 Cor. 5:10). Finally, consider John's special mention of those martyred "because of the Word of God" (Rev. 6:9). They are singled out from all deceased believers at this point in history to receive a white robe (v. 11).

To suffer for the Master is the calling of disciples, whether it ends in martyrdom or not. It is thoroughly biblical to understand the role of suffering for the believer as the gateway to immense blessing from the Father of the Savior, who suffered deeply and was exalted far above every other name (Phil. 2:5–11).

Those who labored in the night shift will praise the name of the Son throughout eternity. Darkness will vanish as these retirees abide in unremitting light.

Come and visit the Night Shift Hall of Fame. See the portraits of these heroes adorning the walls.

The Son's image is, of course, the largest and most central. During His tenure on earth, He was never late for or absent from His nighttime assignment. Retirees who tour the gallery will return again and again to admire His canvas.

However, countless other portraits, each commissioned by the Owner of the vineyard, hang throughout the facility. The Son takes personal pride in each of these canvases and the related stories. Of each He says, "Well done, good and faithful slave. . . . Enter into the joy of your master" (Matt. 25:21).

It is then that we will take special note of William Tyndale, Jeremiah, Hudson Taylor, Moses, Corrie ten Boom, Joseph, D. L. Moody, Jim Elliot, Peter, Martin Luther, Richard Wurmbrand, and the apostle Paul. Room after room contains the likenesses of the afflicted laborers of the heroic night shift.

Consider David, son of Jesse. His portrait attracts many sight-seers to the hall. Having spent an enormous amount of time working under cover of darkness, David was able to respond with wisdom in discovering a sovereign God who was at work in his afflictions.

The Owner specifically drafts the caption for each portrait. Come closer and note the citation under David's portrait:

I waited patiently for the LORD. (Ps. 40:1)

David acquired his attitude of waiting while laboring in the dark. We, too, will develop that same outlook when we find our names on the night shift roster. As our thinking changes, like David's through his night shift experiences, God is able to turn our mourning into dancing (Ps. 30:11).

A night shift prayer:

> *Dear Father, open my eyes to fathom the great work that You are doing through the difficult seasons of my life. Teach me Your ways as You faithfully use my time on the night shift to deepen my roots in Christ. I pray that You would be greatly glorified in my life through the dark experiences that come my way. Amen.*

Seven Stages of the Night-Shift Cycle

Stage One—The Pit

Stage Two—The Wait

Stage Three—The Cry

Stage Four—The Answer

Stage Five—The Deliverance

Stage Six—The New Song

Stage Seven—The Impact

You have put me in the lowest pit,

in dark places, in the depths.

Your wrath has rested upon me,

and You have afflicted me with all Your waves.

Psalm 88:6–7

We are not necessarily doubting that God will do the best for us. We are wondering how painful the best will turn out to be.

C. S. *Lewis*, Letters of C. S. Lewis

Stage One
The Pit

Jeremiah and the Basement Dungeon
(Jer. 37–38)

The year was 588 B.C. Jeremiah was delighted to see the siege of Jerusalem temporarily lifted. Because of the need to shift his troops to fight Egypt on another front, Nebuchadnezzar had abruptly halted the blockade of Jerusalem. This pause in siege activities gave Jeremiah a chance to take care of some real estate business. He packed a few essentials to return the short distance to his family's residence in Anathoth, just outside of Jerusalem, and headed out.

Jeremiah was deep in thought as he walked down the crowded Jerusalem streets. Nearing the gate, he was startled by loud and angry voices. "Traitor! Turncoat!" Glancing in the direction of the strident noise, he realized that taunts and accusations were being hurled at *him*. "You're taking the side of the enemy! Traitor!" It was Irijah, a captain of the king's army, who was accusing Jeremiah. When God commanded the prophet to preach a message that proclaimed the conquest of Jerusalem by Nebuchadnezzar, Jeremiah's obedience provoked the king and much of the Jerusalem populace.

"That's a lie!" Jeremiah retorted. But his emphatic denials were to no avail. Hearing a prophetic message that repeatedly predicted Judah's fall to Babylon, Jeremiah's captors assumed that he was allied with the enemy.

So it was that the prophet Jeremiah was arrested, beaten, and rudely deposited in the dwelling of a scribe named Jonathan. Jonathan's house had been converted into a makeshift prison with a temporary dungeon constructed in the basement for just this kind of situation. Several smaller rooms served as cells. Looking around his filthy cubicle, Jeremiah wondered how he could possibly survive these appalling conditions.

His thoughts turned to the early days. It seemed a very long time ago that he had been recruited, much to his surprise, into prophetic service. A contented "layman," the last thing he had wanted was a job as God's mouthpiece. So Jeremiah resisted the call, but in the end, God prevailed and the reluctant prophet entered ministry. If he had not been convinced of the divine origin of his calling, he could not have survived the abuse and misery of serving the Lord.

The clamor of voices came near, rousing Jeremiah from his musings. How many days had he spent in Jonathan's miserable dungeon? Shivering from the dampness and weak with hunger, he clutched a pathetic rag of a blanket around his shoulders. As he squinted against the light, Jeremiah could see that soldiers from King Zedekiah's royal guard were approaching. "Come!" they commanded, grabbing him and dragging him out into the open.

What a pitiful spectacle he must have made. Haggard, filthy, reeking, and dressed only in tattered rags, he was unfit to stand before decent citizenry, let alone in the presence of a king. But after a hasty bath and a change of clothes, Jeremiah was received by King Zedekiah in the royal court.

Zedekiah was panicky. Appointed by Nebuchadnezzar as a puppet king, he later chose to rebel against him. He was, however, a weak ruler and an ungodly man. In the face of Babylon's bold grab for Jerusalem, Zedekiah knew he was losing control of his kingdom. The siege had created dreadful conditions throughout the city, provisions were scarce, and all feared the looming collapse of the city to Nebuchadnezzar's superior forces.

"Do you have a word from the Lord for me?" Though spiritually unfit, Zedekiah was desperate for some prophetic advice. Since all else had failed, perhaps Jehovah could help.

Jeremiah regarded the monarch with pity. He had constantly given God's Word to Zedekiah, only to be ignored every time. "Why have you thrown me into prison?" Jeremiah responded, his voice breaking. "What is my crime?" Flushed with emotion and weakened by his incarceration, he suddenly snapped. Dropping to his knees, he sobbed uncontrollably. "Oh, please, King Zedekiah," he pled, "please don't send me back to that dungeon. I'll die if you send me back there!"

Moved by this plea, the king granted a reprieve—only to retract it when he was approached by four thugs determined to obtain authorization to put Jeremiah to death. Desperate to hold his disintegrating kingdom intact, he was unable to refuse these ruffians and thus acquiesced to their demands and released Jeremiah to them.

Rushing him away, the four conspirators lowered Jeremiah by ropes into another dungeon belonging to a man called Malchijah. This crude prison was under the same treasury building that housed the courtyard Jeremiah had just left. His cell was actually a pit.

Despair engulfed Jeremiah as his body sank to the cold, muddy bottom. Here vermin, hunger, and the cold would be his solitary companions. At his age, he might quickly get sick and die—that is, if he were lucky!

A faint glimmer of light illuminated the bottom of the well and he slowly inspected his surroundings. The walls were smooth, cut partially out of rock with the remainder earthen. They had been plastered at one time. Looking up, Jeremiah judged he was twenty to twenty-five feet below ground level. His shoulders slumped as he thought of the impossibility of escape. Judging from the mud oozing between his toes, Jeremiah concluded his new home had once been a holding tank for water.

Drifting off to sleep, Jeremiah lost all track of time. He awoke to pale light filtering down the dark shaft and judged that it was evening. In his condition, he couldn't get out of a shallow ditch, let alone this deep cistern. He was completely at the mercy of his enemies. Where was his God now? How could the One who had called him to the prophetic trade so heartlessly abandon him in his time of need?

Meanwhile, God was at work in Zedekiah's court. An Ethiopian named Ebed-melech, with connections in the palace, heard of the prophet's harsh treatment and intervened. This time the king responded favorably. "Take thirty men and get Jeremiah out," the king directed. "Return him to the treasury building."

Due to Jeremiah's condition, special measures were needed to bring him up from the pit. Ebed-melech and his aides let down old rags and worn-out clothes with ropes, and then instructed Jeremiah to use those to pad the ropes to protect his arms as they pulled him out. By evening, he had been returned, unharmed, to the courtyard prison, where he remained until the fall of Jerusalem in 586 B.C.

A Tale of Two Sufferers

This detailed account of Jeremiah's story provides unexpected insight into the afflictions of a man of God. Jeremiah is Everyman and the pit is for every Christian—though the pit experience itself will differ for each. However, since only a modest number of believers will ever find themselves imprisoned in vermin-infested cisterns, it might be easy to catalog Jeremiah's experience as atypical, an aberration in the history of night shift appointments.

Not so. As a truck driver for a heating oil distributor, I was often called upon to deliver fuel oil to homes I had never served before. These visits were frequently lessons from God to illustrate some aspect of the muck and gloom of Jeremiah's pit. Stopping one day to service one particular home, I rapidly concluded that the residents were dog owners. The backyard was a pathetic plot of ground totally carpeted with canine excrement. Not one bare spot existed on which to place my foot. A nauseating stench permeated the air.

This particular delivery necessitated parking my truck in the front, dragging my hose along the side of the house to the rear, and entering the backyard to deposit oil in the fill pipe near the back porch. Fortunately for my sanity, I did not have to walk through the entire length of the yard to do my job.

Unfortunately, it was impossible to enter and leave unscathed. By the time I finished providing the heating oil needs of these people, I had acquired an impressive quantity of dog droppings on my clothing and gear.

Returning to my truck in a sour mood, I began the task of rewinding the hose. Relief swept over me at the thought that I would soon be far away from this awful place. With one hand I pushed the rewind button, keeping the other firmly on the hose to guide it onto the reel. During this procedure, I was revulsed to observe dog excrement trickling between my fingers. The fact that I was wearing gloves did not lessen my disgust.

After rewinding the hose, I inspected my pants and shirt. I had begun the day as a model employee—shaven, hair combed, uniform ironed—eager to make a good impression. I now appeared and smelled as if I had slept in a dog kennel.

My emotions were often raw as I went about my oil delivery rounds. As a former pastor, I was in a state of perpetual bewilderment and semi-anger at the strange direction the Divine Finger had pointed in placing me here. Consequently, it was a continuous battle to maintain my spiritual and emotional equilibrium.

At this moment I was outraged. How dare these people expose me to such a vile situation! I didn't deserve this kind of treatment! Only a few months earlier, I had been a minister. I had preached sermons, counseled the troubled, and done the work of the Lord. Now I was being forced to work in dog excrement. For this I had gone to seminary?

Stained and struggling, I was Samuel, sword in hand, eager to hew King Agag to pieces (1 Sam. 15:33). Oh, how I longed to see the occupants of this house step innocently out onto their front porch for just a brief moment. They would be shocked to see a frenzied truck driver, pupils dilated, neck veins bulging. In righteous vengeance I would charge them, nozzle in hand, spewing seventy gallons of the golden liquid every minute.

Fortunately for all, God is good and the residents maintained their invisibility. My anger gradually subsided. I continued on my route for the balance of the day, noticing that my remaining customers kept more distance than usual between us as I made my rounds.

The nagging irritation of this dilemma lingered with me for many days. Like Jeremiah, the contrast between my calling and reality could not have been greater. First, God had chosen to place me in full-time pastoral ministry for a number of years. Then I was moved from a pastoral ministry to a life of personal discouragement, exposed to gross indignities. Seething within was deep resentment toward all involved: former deacons and elders, my current employer and supervisor, my oil delivery customers, and, of course, God.

Yes, I was most angry with God, for it was He who had taken a young man seeking to serve Him in pastoral ministry and transferred him to such an appalling situation. Like David, with Saul's spear vibrating next to his head, my compensation for faithfulness was an unwanted career change; wretched night shift chores my only reward for obedience to the divine call.

The Cost of the Call

This matter of *calling* is important to all believers. I, like Jeremiah, was a "reluctant prophet." Working in pastoral ministry was not my career-of-choice as a young man. God fingered me when I was planning to do other things. In return, I had no alternative but to consent to do His bidding. How peculiar this God who calls hesitant preachers and then complicates their profession beyond belief! One would expect the vineyard Owner to give His workers the easiest of paths since they are only trying to obey Him.

Instead, two decades into a difficult and painful assignment, God uprooted me, reassigned me to an oil truck, and layered me with dog excrement. Jeremiah unambiguously teaches us that our approach to serving the Lord must be nuanced by the realities of ministry and the cost that God exacts of His servants, lest we faint along the way.

This truth was reinforced for me a few years ago. While attending a graduation ceremony for Christian high school seniors, I heard a testimony that still echoes in my ears. A youthful, pink-faced senior rose to share his post-graduation plans. I remember him sagely intoning, "Well, I've been accepted at Bible college. I'll be preparing for the pastoral ministry and eventually I'll plant a church in Eastern Europe."

Don't get me wrong. I'm thrilled when young people want to serve the Lord. But, oh, the seeming glibness of such words from an eighteen-year-old rookie as they land on the cauliflower ears of ministers who have spent mega-time sparring with God in the dark. Seated in the audience, I thought, *My, such an erudite testimony, but I fear he may not have a clue what he's talking about.*

As he spoke earnestly of his calling, I squirmed in my seat, my mind flashing back to hard-charging Moses in pursuit of his dream (Ex. 2:11–15). Haunting images of some well-intentioned but disastrous experiences early in my own ministry flashed across my mental screen. I visualized this high school senior himself someday slaying an Egyptian and fleeing to Midian in a cloud of dust, his dreams dashed and his resources depleted. Or what if he found himself, like Jeremiah, rudely deposited in some sodden pit?

I was seized with a tremendous urge to rise from my chair, rush to the platform, and stop this young man before he did some serious damage. Picture the scene as I shook him vigorously, all the while squawking: "Have you lost your mind, boy? Don't you dare talk about going into the ministry unless Almighty God Himself grabs you by the nape of the neck and compels you!" I would then cuff him on the ear (euphemistically, of course) and tell him to go study business or science or education.

The truth is that I wisely resisted this impulse and remained seated. My wife, sitting next to me, understands these things. She, too, has been profoundly buffeted by the winds of pastoral "fate." We exchanged knowing smiles.

And so it is with those whom God calls. First, people who understand the magnitude of God's summons should be like Moses or Jeremiah—initially hesitant to respond—for the cost has always been significant for those who choose to obey God's bidding. Second, any calling is a calling to God's Word. No message is relevant unless rooted in the revealed Word of God. Third, because of God's Word, it is a vocation of suffering. After all, God's foes hate His voice. And, fourth, it is a passionate occupation, for the Word will sear our hearts within. Spoken or not, the revealed Word of God will be a fire ignited by the Holy Spirit, which will burn the heart of its bearer (Jer. 20:9).

This is the beginning of the "pit cycle," that recurring season of life for true servants of the Lord. It is a difficult time because humans dislike suffering and inconvenience. But what abundant fruit is produced by those who endure, for the benefit is brokenness and usefulness to the Master!

Dungeons and Other Dark Places

The Psalms present this dilemma (what the Bible often calls "the pit") in a variety of graphic terms: *bees, bulls, bow and arrow, dark, disease, dogs, dry (arid) land, earthquake, famine, fire, foxes, grave, hunger and thirst, homelessness, lions, mud, narrowness, net, pestilence, prison, serpents, snare, sword, war, waters,* and *wild oxen.* This partial listing suggests the rich vocabulary available to the psalmist in describing the predicament that often confronts those who desire to serve the Lord.

We may experience the night shift in many ways. For instance, we may have a desire to do one thing while God is calling us to do something quite different. Or as we begin to serve Him, He may appear disinterested in our efforts. Sometimes it may seem He allows obstacles while doing nothing to remove them.

At other times we may recognize and seek to use the gifts God has given us for ministry, only to have the door closed in our face before we even have an opportunity to exercise them.

In the Bible, two features of the pit bear special emphasis: *narrowness* and *the fear of man.* First, the pit is a place of constriction or narrowness. The literal Hebrew word for *narrow* is often translated "distress." Notice the following:

Answer me when I call, O God of my righteousness! You have *relieved* me in my *distress*; be gracious to me and hear my prayer (Ps. 4:1).

The words *relieved* and *distress* form a wordplay in this verse. A marginal note in a study Bible may indicate that the word *relieved* here means "to broaden" or "make room for." Since we know that this word *distress* usually refers to narrowness, we may rightly translate the second line of Psalm 4:1 in this way: "You have broadened me in my narrowness."

David often felt that he was in a place of "spiritual claustrophobia":

The cords of death encompassed me, and the torrents of ungodliness terrified me. The cords of Sheol surrounded me; the snares of death confronted me. In my distress I called upon the LORD (Ps. 18:4–6a).

Many bulls have surrounded me; strong bulls of Bashan have encircled me.... For dogs have surrounded me; a band of evildoers has encompassed me (Ps. 22:12, 16).

All nations surrounded me; in the name of the LORD I will surely cut them off. They surrounded me, yes, they surrounded me; in the name of the LORD I will surely cut them off. They surrounded me like bees; they were extinguished as a fire of thorns; in the name of the LORD I will surely cut them off (Ps. 118:10–12).

The pit allowed life to close in on David, and it will do the same for you. The pit limits your options and restricts your freedom. You cannot do what you want to do when you are in the pit. Even the positive results of ministry—financial freedom, good health, blissful marriage and home life, vocational success, fulfilling church life—all become constricted on the night shift and you are left alone with God and your quandary.

These night shift texts reveal the mind-set of the one who is "narrowed." We might ask ourselves, *What did David want to do?* The answer, of course, would be that he wanted to live and to reign as king. Obviously, at the moment, David couldn't be king and his life was constantly threatened. Thus, the pit constricted him and he was incapable of stretching and moving as he wished. Fortunately, David eventually would be "broadened." But for now we are left to contemplate the frustrating predicament of the one who is called by God while simultaneously prevented from fulfilling that calling. This is true narrowness, genuine distress.

Second, those who enter the pit are afraid of what man can do to them, and so the pit experience is needed to rid them of that fear. The fear of man (a mind-set to unlearn) and the fear of the Lord (an attitude to obtain) are vivid themes in Scripture. The first is natural; the second, acquired.

In Psalm 118, the psalmist is apparently recounting the greatness of the God who delivered him from a pit experience. Note that he describes this experience as "distress" (v. 5). Further, we discover that he has been moved to a "broad place." This move having been accomplished, what lessons might the psalmist relate to us?

> The LORD is for me; I will not fear; what can man do to me? The LORD is for me among those who help me; therefore I will look with satisfaction on those who hate me. It is better to take refuge in the LORD than to trust in man. It is better to take refuge in the LORD than to trust in princes (Ps. 118:6-9).

When fleeing from Absalom, David wrote these words:

> I will not be afraid of ten thousands of people who have set themselves against me round about (Ps. 3:6).

The fear of man is one of the most crippling aspects of our humanity as we seek to serve the Lord. I must confess that the fear of man was one of the key ingredients of my deep malaise and spiritual depression early in my thirty-month pit experience in 1991. Having left the comfort zone of professional ministry in which I had labored for almost two decades, there was a subconscious pressure that I must continue in the ministry in order to be respected and to support my family. I had no other calling and few marketable skills.

But the doors began to slam around me. Good people—fine Christian leaders, all—examined my resumé, interviewed me, and then turned elsewhere. Not knowing that God had already consulted with Himself and determined that I needed a season on the night shift, I became frustrated, angry, and, yes, afraid.

I mistakenly concluded that humans held the key to my ministry and my future. My eyes were on people, and a season of labor in the dark was necessary to teach me the hard lessons that David, Jeremiah, Moses, John the Baptist, Joseph, yes, even Jesus, had to learn at night. The Owner's plan was for me to graduate from Night School knowing the fear of the Lord.

Seven Stages of the Night Shift Cycle

One who enters the pit crosses the threshold to "God's turf." This entrance sets in motion a cycle of events and activities designed to transform proud, unbroken, and essentially useless people into vibrant servants of Christ who have a new song on their lips, a message to proclaim, and a usefulness in making an impact for the Kingdom.

This cycle, a persistent topic throughout Scripture, is a biblical process portrayed in seven stages. They are:

1. The Pit—the miserable place of testing and brokenness.

2. The Wait—the period of time one is forced to spend on the night shift, lingering there at God's pleasure, often without divine explanation.

3. The Cry—the desperate prayer of the one who is forced to wait in the pit.

4. The Answer—God's response to the sufferer as He opens His Word and reveals the message that is to be the core of future ministry.

5. The Deliverance—the glorious liberation of the suffering servant in God's way, God's timing, and for God's purpose.

6. The New Song—the music inspired by freedom from the fear of man that produces true delight in God alone.

7. The Impact—the usefulness that comes to the one who allows the season of suffering to do its work.

To understand the night shift cycle, we start at the beginning. The pit was where I began to understand the strange nature of God's summons. To the young, calls from God are exciting and challenging. When the Lord beckoned me in my early twenties, I did not comprehend what demands would be placed on me, nor what volleys of pain and injury would bombard me. Never having heard of "God's night shift," I didn't imagine that He would so thoroughly bludgeon me under cover of darkness. Apparently Jeremiah experienced similar shock, for he said:

O LORD, You have deceived me and I was deceived; You have overcome me and prevailed. I have become a laughingstock all day long; everyone mocks me (Jer. 20:7).

Make no mistake about it; Jeremiah's frustration was with God. No one else got the blame for his predicament except the One who called him.

Our agreement to follow Jesus Christ is a pact to serve Him for the rest of our lives. Generally, however, the new recruit has no idea of the price that the journey may exact. The night shift axiom goes this way: *Our natural goal is comfort. God's goal is to make us useful for His glory. To attain His goal, God interferes with ours.*

You and other readers represent a multiplicity of callings. You need not be in vocational Christian ministry or pastoral work to have an authentic calling, nor do you need to be in full-time ministry to be assigned to the night shift. Your calling may be as a godly mother, father, construction laborer, secretary, grandparent, Sunday school teacher, choir director, neighbor, youth worker, or medical professional. And your night shift assignment may touch any number of aspects of your life. As we each pursue God's appointment for our lives, the threat of a night shift assignment looms ominously ahead as one inevitable dimension of God's calling.

There are a variety of potential night shift experiences for the people of God. See if you can find yours listed in this catalog of possibilities:

- trapped in a stale or lonely marriage
- suffocated by a dead-end career
- despairing over rebellious children
- burdened by deteriorating health
- surviving the death of a loved one
- strapped by mounting bills with little income
- defeated by educational failure
- humiliated by criticism and rejection
- discouraged by childlessness
- betrayed by a friend
- oppressed by the dark gloom of clinical depression
- frustrated by a ministry that appears to be going nowhere
- arriving at old age and feeling useless
- addicted and helpless to overcome the addiction
- single but yearning for a spouse

This random index can give the person in the pit a flavor for the broader dimensions of the night shift under God's direction. We are all slated for seasons when we find our name on the night shift roster.

"Get Me Out of Here!"

Perhaps the most distinctive attribute of a true biblical pit experience is the discovery that one can do little to remedy the situation. The pit is too deep, too strong, too wide, too overwhelming. One who is in the pit is truly stuck there!

In my own pit season, the most troubling aspect of all was that I was no longer in command. Another Person overruled me at every turn as I found myself strangely crying out for autonomy. My frustrations mounted because, according to my reasoning, my seminary training and teaching gifts could be better used in another venue to further God's work.

During this time of affliction, well-meaning friends advised me that I should rejoice in my secular jobs, for this was the will of God for me. One kind friend suggested that I was a poor testimony because I didn't like my work! This kind of counsel is generally well intended, and I needed to hear it, for it contained an element of truth and a dimension of caution. However, such guidance did not account for the dynamics of the pit experience or for my calling from God.

The night shift sojourn is an exceptional period. While it is right and proper to be thankful at all times, even in the pit, the lessons being taught under cover of darkness can make thankfulness a secondary matter. Sometimes we are given suffering to *learn to be thankful.* The darkness has the power to temporarily minimize all joy and hope. An understanding Savior, the Great Sufferer of the universe, realizes the vineyard laborer, whose burden already seems too much to bear, should not be expected to carry additional burdens. There is a time and a place to learn each lesson. Gratitude and joy may come much later. For now, other lessons must be learned in the dark so we can emerge into the light with true gratitude. A grateful response may temporarily elude the pit sojourner who is under the heavy teaching hand of God.

I had absolutely no control over my circumstances while that Invisible Hand kept a tight grip on me. Every attempt to remedy my situation failed. This is the essence of the pit of Psalm 40: Changes in circumstances are subject to God's choice, not mine.

*   *   *

Greg is a great friend who, along with his wife, understands the pit quite well. We met almost thirty years ago while I was coaching basketball in college. A likable, witty fellow, Greg was an outstanding athlete, popular with everyone.

During his college years, my friend had insomnia and a resultant low energy level. His problems intensified as the years passed so that it is now almost impossible for him to undertake any kind of regular vocational activity. His days have been marked by cycles of deep depression, overpowering fatigue, suicidal impulses, lack of clarity of thought, loss of power to concentrate, and plenty of apprehension about his future. He is seeing his aspiration to serve the Lord in full-time ministry constantly undermined by the realities of his physical condition.

Added to these problems are frequent doctor and hospital visits, with the financial burdens incurred. Through God's miraculous provision and the creative financial management and frugality of his wife, Lynn, Greg's family presses on.

Compounding these difficulties is the hereditary nature of his physical problems and the discovery that he has passed his ailments on to two of his children, who are already under medical care. Lynn has been a stalwart through these stressful years. Faithful and trusting to the end, she has endured the night shift by faithfulness to her marriage vows and her commitment to Christ. As Greg and Lynn pass the age of fifty, they have spent much of their married life on the vineyard night shift. Their personal dreams largely unfulfilled, both are nevertheless faithfully serving the Lord under cover of darkness.

Both Greg and Lynn are preparing themselves for the real probability that the rest of their vineyard labors may very well be characterized by a perpetual pit experience. Their names may not be removed from the night shift roster this side of "Retirement" to heaven. There, I imagine the Son will lead a tour through the Night Shift Hall of Fame. Wandering through the corridors, we will stop at Greg and Lynn's portrait. The Son will smile and point to the caption that He Himself has recorded: "Good and Faithful Servants."

Purpose for the Pit

It is not enough to say that the pit "happens." No, night shift assignments are essential to God's goals. This is why the night shift contexts are found throughout the Psalms. While we may think that affliction for God's servants is the exception, not the rule, the testimony of Scripture would deny that assumption. If God's work is to be done, He will choose to do much of it "on the night shift."

The Owner has two main objectives for assigning laborers to this shift. The first is *long-range and external*, involving groups of people and the larger goals that God intends to accomplish in the world. In sending the great missionary statesman Hudson Taylor home to England from his beloved China because of back problems, God demonstrated this first purpose. The sudden change of address came at a time when Taylor's ministry in China needed him most, or so he thought. Taylor endured a year of bed rest in traction to treat his back problem, a circumstance he judged to be a horrendous setback to the expansion of the Gospel in China.

For one year, Hudson Taylor could do nothing but pray. Taylor spent the year asking God to raise up one hundred replacements to go to China. At the end of that year he saw the answer to his prayers! By removing Taylor from day work, assigning him to the night shift, and forcing him into a period of "inactivity," God accomplished a greater work.

In parallel to Hudson Taylor's experience, the great Chicago fire of October 1871 actually broke out while the eminent evangelist Dwight L. Moody was in the middle of a sermon. As the flames erupted, the congregation fled the meeting in panic. Before the blaze was extinguished, 2,100 acres and 17,450 buildings were destroyed, 250 people burned to death, and 150,000 were made homeless. Among the smoldering ruins left by the inferno were Moody's new home, his new church building, and a meeting hall he had recently constructed.

Moody remembered the following year as a time of intense chastening in his life. But in the aftermath of the fire, God touched him in a new and fresh way. Under cover of darkness, God worked in Moody to move him to a new level of effectiveness. The darkness of the night shift proved a turning point in his ministry.

David was frustrated by life as a fugitive. Jeremiah was miserable in his dungeon sojourn. Moody was chastened by fire. Charles Spurgeon suffered enormous physical ailments and depression. Hudson Taylor was beset with back problems. Greg and Lynn continue to have their particular afflictions. And I was immeasurably disheartened with my oil delivery assignment when I wanted to be preaching the Word of God. Yet each of these pit experiences was instrumental in propelling servants of the Lord forward through newly opened doors of ministry.

"Lord, What Are You Doing?"

God's second objective in allowing His children to enter the pit involves *internal needs*—what He is doing in us more than His accomplishments through us. This purpose produces an internal course adjustment that gives us a quantum surge in our outlook on God, ourselves, and the world around us.

In Psalm 40, this transformed outlook is given in one phrase of verse 3: "He put a new song in my mouth." While the "new song" will be the focus of Stage Six of the night shift cycle, the point must be made here that the song is new and it is learned in the dark. For those who want to learn the new music of the Kingdom Vineyard, music lessons on the night shift are indispensable.

But the pit is also mysterious; it produces questions that besiege us. While we are in the pit, we are prone to God-analysis, instinctively playing amateur theologian as the Owner pulls out the divine clipboard and makes His baffling roster changes. Perhaps Jeremiah may have reasoned that, if he could just understand what God was doing, he could better cooperate with Him in the dungeon and wait patiently for Him to be done.

The actual truth may be less flattering to us: the more we scrutinize God's night shift activities, the more we may interfere with Him! Usually our curiosity receives no response during a night shift tenure, producing a key axiom: God characteristically does not divulge His mysterious plans to those who are in the darkness.

When I entered this season, I had a rudimentary understanding of night shift principles. I knew that God was at work, that His plan for me would be positive, that He loved me, and that He would always be faithful to me. As a pastor I had taught such truths to others because I believed them. But God did not necessarily intend for the knowledge of such truth to lessen the sharp edge of night labor.

While the morning crew may speak of blessings, haggle over the finer points of doctrine, and chat about the weather, a fresh sincerity and depth characterizes the conversations of workers in the darkness. Just as the instruction that a recruit receives in boot camp may hold little relevance to the untried soldier, nevertheless, in the thick of battle that same Marine will frantically try to remember the training received so casually months earlier.

When one is on the day shift, leisurely discourse about the Bible is a luxury. However, when seeking refuge from a fusillade of afflictions, the teaching of God's Word becomes the means of survival. There is no time for doctrinal pettiness, theological sloppiness, and biblical shallowness. The need for truth is compelling; in the pit there is no time for Bible Trivia!

So it was my experience that for many months there was no heavenly explanation as to why I was in my current "predicament" while other believers (and pastors) seemed to have fewer problems. I gained no insight as to whether or not I would ever return to full-time ministry. There were no audible heavenly voices reassuring me that all was well and that things would make sense in the end. I recurrently lacked even the basic confidence that God remembered me and was sovereignly managing my affairs.

Entering God's Waiting Room

Each morning I would arise, spend time meditating on Psalm 40, and proceed to my appointed duties for the day with a knot in the pit of my stomach. Like Jeremiah and other men and women of faith, I sought to obey against my feelings while waiting for God to break through into space and time with answers and a new assignment for me. Whether delivering oil, driving tour buses, or mowing lawns, my mind would inevitably return to these deeper questions, and I would find myself crying out to God for a shift transfer.

In the Information Age, we have ready access to immense quantities of data. With most details no further away than our fingertips, it makes no sense that should we be in the dark about what God is up to in our lives. Yet there remains a dearth of answers for the sojourner in the pit. If the "why" question could be answered during the pit experience, the pit would lose its teaching power, for it is when there are no answers, when things seem meaningless, that we are most attentive. The pit grips us precisely for this reason: it is largely baffling until release comes.

When this principle is understood and affirmed, the power and necessity of "waiting on God" becomes clear, as it did for David and Jeremiah and Hudson Taylor and Greg and Lynn and countless others.

And, of course, Moses. . . .

* * *

A prayer from the pit:

Heavenly Father, You have wisely allowed pit experiences to come my way. Oh, how I hate these afflictions! I believe that You, in Your sovereignty, could have prevented them. Perhaps someday I will understand why You permitted them. For now, though, I trust You, knowing that You never make mistakes. In Jesus' name, Amen.

How long, O Lord?

Will You forget me forever?

How long will You hide Your face from me?

How long shall I take counsel in my soul,

having sorrow in my heart all the day?

How long will my enemy be exalted over me?

Psalm 13:1–2

My times are in Your hand.

Psalm 31:15

STAGE TWO
THE WAIT

Moses and Eighty "Wasted" Years
(Ex. 2:16–3:12)

Baaaaa. Moses' head jerked up at the sound of a lamb's bleat-ing. While resting in the shade of a rock outcropping, he had dozed off in the desert heat. Stretching his muscles, Moses surveyed the pastoral scene around him, his thoughts drifting back over the years. It didn't seem so very long ago that he had fled Egypt in the middle of the night. Since then, forty years had raced by. In retrospect, Moses' ill-fated attempts at delivering his people from Egypt's bondage seemed like a bad dream.

Even in his youth, when he had first unearthed the truth about his family background, a smoldering passion had sustained him. Eventually the embers had been fanned into a blazing fire. Confident of his abilities, he had spent every waking hour planning for the day when he would lead his people to freedom.

In a reflective mood, it seemed that from the vantage point of the Midian wilderness and forty years of contemplation, trying to kill the Egyptians off one by one was an absurd strategy for liberating his people! But forty years ago, when he was vigorous and naive, things had looked a whole lot different. Only after he had killed the Egyptian was flight the lone sensible option.

Upon his arrival in Midian, Moses' plan had been to seclude himself for a while before returning to Egypt for another try at leading a Hebrew revolt. Day after day Moses' heart burned for the emancipation of his people. But slowly, as the years drifted by, the flame of vision ebbed until it was all but extinguished. Now it hurt too much to think about his personal failure and his kinsmen still in slavery. He was a shepherd now.

As a herder, content with his lot, Moses was reconciled to caring for his father-in-law's flocks for the rest of his life. At this point, he simply refused to think about Goshen, his fellow Hebrews, and the passion that had once kept him awake at night. He was an old man with no vision, little ambition, and dwindling energy.

Moses sniffed the acrid air. It was the smell of smoke. Glancing around, he noticed that a small brush fire had erupted nearby. He had seen these kinds of blazes before, a common sight in the burning heat of the desert. More out of curiosity and boredom than for any other reason, Moses strolled over in the direction of the flames. *Hmmmm*, he thought. *There is something peculiar about this bush....*

The Mystery of God's Clock

We enter the divine laboratory, eager to comprehend the obscure. Our test case: Moses. The assignment: To decipher the timetable God employs when working with His children. For our analysis, we will analyze Moses' Day-Timer as a grand illustration of the "pit wait" described in Psalm 40:1.

The Scriptures offer us rich biographical insight on the issue of protracted time spent on the night shift. For all who have not experienced eternity, God's calendar is shrouded in secrecy, causing one to wonder just how God computes time anyway. A failure to understand His concept of human waiting will prevent the servant-in-training from learning necessary lessons on the night shift.

To the afflicted one, time drags on and on. In his youth,

Moses had undoubtedly thought he was going somewhere and that he needed to get there "now." God's response: "Not so fast!"

The Hebrew text of Psalm 40:1, written by David, gives the insider's view of "the wait," the opening phrase being translatable as: "I waited intensely for Yahweh." *Intense waiting* is a fitting rendition of this phrase. Unfortunately, our major Bible translations insert the word *patiently* immediately following *waited*, suggesting a leisurely pause in David's stressful life. We might picture David in his lawn chair, sunglasses resting on the bridge of his nose. He is sipping iced tea outside of the cave of Adullam and doing a crossword puzzle ("across" would be right to left in Hebrew, of course) while he "patiently" waits for God to get around to him.

Such is definitely *not* the case with the biblical "wait." The Hebrew text of Psalm 40:1 conveys the notion of a protracted, concentrated kind of waiting. Make no mistake about it—the delay David remembers was a grueling marathon, one that exacted an enormous toll in terms of time, emotion, resources, and energy. When one waits on the night shift, hardship will ensue, banishing the word *patient* from the "waiter's" vocabulary.

A recent doctor's appointment underscored this principle for me. No part of the medical world may be more aptly named than the doctor's "waiting room." When trying to see a doctor, often all one can do is wait. Although there are punctual physicians, many doctors seem to operate on their own timetable.

My appointment was for 1 P.M. Arriving fifteen minutes early, I filled out some papers and was told to "wait." After a season of unexplained waiting, I asked the nurse if she knew how much longer before the doctor would see me. "Maybe another fifteen minutes," she said. Perhaps I was wrong, but I thought I saw a mysterious twinkle in her eye.

Having gone outside for ten minutes or so, I returned to the doctor's office at 2 P.M. I again inquired of the nurse who, more honestly, told me that she had no idea how long it would be. I left, never seeing that doctor.

I was troubled that the doctor assumed that he owed his waiting patients no explanation for the extreme delay. Since I knew that he was in the examining room with other patients, my frustration over my wasted time was heightened. It was not merely his lateness that offended me; I fully understood the interruptions that can occur in a doctor's schedule. Still, any reasonable excuse or attempt at explanation would have lessened my irritation over the inconvenience.

The Divine Cold Shoulder

Unbroken silence is often the most exasperating aspect of The Wait. To most Westerners, time is a precious form of currency. Unlike money, however, we cannot create more time. We can only try to manage the uniform allotment we all receive. So the need to wait without explanation and without communication is to allow others to waste our most precious resources.

My doctor, much like God, used his time allocation as he saw fit while forcing his patients to "waste" some of their quota of this precious asset. This strange perspective on time is implied by the statement, "With the Lord one day is like a thousand years, and a thousand years like one day" (2 Pet. 3:8). When God controls the clock, we are bewildered as we try to compute a proper length for our night shift assignment.

Additionally, as if to compound our annoyance, our God does not make a habit of informing us of His timetable when we're on this shift. We might expect a loving God, like any devoted parent, to communicate freely with His children. So we are surprised to receive no specific information from Him as to our status.

David understood "the divine cold shoulder." Having been anointed by Samuel to replace Saul, David spent an extraordinary amount of time running from the king in an effort to stay alive. A conservative chronology of 1 Samuel 16–31 suggests that David exhausted at least a decade, perhaps as many as fifteen or twenty years, running from Saul as a fugitive in his own country.

After a particularly close call with death, David went to visit Samuel (1 Sam. 19:18). We are not privy to the details of their conversation, only informed that David advised Samuel of Saul's treatment of him. I wouldn't be surprised if David didn't say something like this: "Come on, Samuel! This is ridiculous. Can't I just go back to tending sheep? You anointed me to be the next king and then my life fell apart. I've had nothing but trouble since you visited Bethlehem, and I'm sick of it. And another thing, my walk with the Lord used to be a delight. Now, when my troubles are at their peak, God doesn't seem to be telling me anything. I didn't ask for this, Samuel."

No, we don't know what David said, nor do we have any idea how Samuel might have responded. Unquestionably, the wait exacted an enormous price from David during those fugitive years. This appears to be God's way.

Even Jesus shocked His disciples by dozing in the boat in the midst of a raging storm. *Surely He should be awake and intervening on our behalf*, they must have thought. Instead, Jesus was stunned by their display of fear and unbelief (Luke 8:22-25). Loved but seemingly ignored by a silent God, we simply wait and wait and wait.

Here may well be the most startling statement in the Bible: "You do not answer!" (Ps. 22:2). These four words make the night shift nearly intolerable. We say, "I can endure anything as long as I can hear God talking to me." Then we're stunned to discover that, in the midst of our deepest trials, He seems to *stop* talking. David makes a connection between God's silence and the pit experience when he says, "Do not be deaf to me, for if You are silent to me, I will become like those who go down to the pit" (Ps. 28:1). When the voice of God is not heard, one is truly under cover of darkness.

And yet, since God cannot be rude, this "divine cold shoulder" belies the fact that He carefully guards our time and uses it for good. Since Psalm 88 calls the pit "the land of forgetfulness," we should not be surprised when we feel forgotten. This is a vital component of the Night School curriculum.

Also, unlike doctors, only God's view of time counts. Since He is the Sovereign Lord, we must acknowledge His right to use our allotment of time as He sees fit. This supply of time that we so jealously hoard and dispense was given to us by Him and must be unstintingly relinquished back to Him.

Consider an excerpt from my journal, dated May 29, 1993:

I hate our life right now and everything about it. It's all a mess and I can hardly stand it. No church or ministry has the slightest interest in us. God is silent! It's as if I have the plague. Everything is dark. I can get my hopes up but as time drags by, it's clear that I was dreaming.

The ironic feature of this particular journal entry is the date. As I was penning these melancholic words, unbeknownst to me, the church that God was preparing for me to pastor was entering its own night shift. That church and I both spent the summer of 1993 working in the darkness, but by fall we would jointly receive a sort of day shift roster reassignment.

Neither David nor Moses nor any other person who has ever truly waited on God is likely to endure His Waiting Room with a lighthearted attitude. Waiting is miserable work. It goes against the grain of our personalities and culture. In an "instant society," patient waiting seems almost un-American. And patient I was not!

The Long Way Home

Let's compare two adjacent verses of Scripture. First, "It is eleven days' journey from Horeb by the way of Mount Seir unto Kadesh-barnea" (Deut. 1:2). Then notice the very next verse: "In the fortieth year . . ." (v. 3).

Ironically, these two verses frame the bulk of Moses' ministry to the Children of Israel. This comment in Scripture is intended to serve as more than a road map in case one decides to make the trip up the peninsula from Horeb (or Mount Sinai) to Kadesh-barnea. Actually, it is the divine timetable in the form of a Heavenly Highway Atlas. Moses may check the figures as often as he wishes, but the result is always the same. An eleven-day trip takes forty years. Hmmm . . .

What happened between verses two and three? Instead of marching Israel into Canaan in eleven days, God took them on a route that exacted a hefty toll from Moses and the people he was leading. The wilderness experience of the sons of Israel is one of the exceptional night shift stories in Scripture. After waiting forty years in Midian, Moses had his comfortable life disrupted by a burning bush. Then it took another forty years to accomplish an eleven-day journey.

I've often wondered about the conversation Moses and God might have had concerning the route God chose. *Sinai to Kadesh-barnea via Mount Seir Highway*, thought Moses, planning Israel's trip. *Eleven days. It'll be a piece of cake. Let's get going!* However, after he consulted with the Divine AAA Trip Service, picture Moses again with his Sinai-Canaan road atlas spread out before him on the sand. He pores over the charts, thumbing through various scrolls, examining mileage data. Muttering under his breath, he is clearly perplexed at the route God has directed him to take. "Wait a minute!" he blurts out, rapidly punching some mileage figures into his calculator. He checks and rechecks his computations.

Finally exasperated, he says, "Lord, I'm sorry, but this is highly irregular! Just look at the circuitous route You've chosen for us. You know this peninsula far better than I do, but the thought of wandering around with this bunch any longer than necessary is more than I can bear. Now, how about this straight shot north? I can get them there in, oh, say, about eleven days."

At that point, Moses would have expected a response from God. Our silent God may have simply refused to elaborate on His reasons. Or, He might have said, "I understand, Moses. You're right. But take some extra time for the trip, anyway." End of discussion. Moses has much to tell us about waiting on God, doesn't he?

The Waiting Game

Moses' example quickly shatters one of our illusions about the Christian life: the idea that "waiting on God" is leisurely, inactive, passive, and undemanding. The phrase "waiting on God" has sometimes been used in a specialized way, as if to describe a *personal decision* one has made to take no further steps until God clearly directs. Actually, when one is on the night shift, the laborer has no choice regarding waiting. In the darkness, no one casually says, "I think I'll wait on God."

Because this shift has so many unpleasant dimensions, we will want an immediate change of assignment. "Give me better hours!" we demand of the Owner of Kingdom Vineyard. "Put me back on the day shift!" In the words of the psalmist, this may sound something like, "How long, O Lord?" But only the Owner fully understands the needs and demands of meeting the vineyard production objectives. So, using His "secret formula," He composes an updated night shift roster, assigning and moving workers as He deems fit. The person assigned to the darkness is incapable of self-delivery. This person must show up for work in the dark until the Owner changes His mind! Waiting brings us to the point where we can say, "My times are in Your hand" (Ps. 31:15). In the pit, our calendar is relinquished to the One whose hands are big enough for our times.

In the shadows of Midian, Moses reflected on the reality that doing things his way had led to defeat in Egypt. As a miserable failure, he had fled for his life, abandoning his noble vision. He could not deliver the Hebrew people from their Egyptian bondage, so flight or capture were his only choices.

Once in the desert, the shepherd's life, marriage, and fatherhood provided him with a diversion and gave direction to his life. Like most men and women who suffer severe disappointment in their past, recollections of his failure were too painful for Moses. The vision gradually faded until Egypt and the Hebrew people were a faint image. Moses eased his pained memory by immersing himself in his new life, family, and vocation.

The Bible is absolutely silent regarding the time between Moses' arrival in Midian and the burning bush altar call. What took place between God and Moses under cover of darkness? Did God speak to the Midian shepherd during those forty years on the night shift? Was Moses listening? Did Moses speak to God? Did He answer? Fascinating questions with few concrete answers.

Jesus' words on the cross emphasize the abandonment that He perceived during His own dark night of the soul: "My God, my God, why have You forsaken me?" (Ps. 22:1; Matt. 27:46). Jesus (and David) know what it's like to cry to the Father at the darkest hour of the night shift and get no reply:"I cry by day, but You do not answer; and by night, but I have no rest" (Ps. 22:2).

Rather than being amazed that we hear very little from God during our night shift rotation, perhaps we should be startled if He speaks at all. While divine silence is undoubtedly the most frustrating and outstanding peculiarity defining the biblical pit experience, it may also be the most potent teaching tool in God's arsenal. His tight-lipped approach to His night crew should tell us something about God's pedagogical methods.

One thing is painfully clear. When God eventually did speak to Moses, the old shepherd had little interest in recovering the old dream. Playing the waiting game in Midian, Moses might have arrived at some sort of mutual understanding with God:"Okay, You won't talk to me, so I won't talk to You." Having grown accustomed to God's silence, Moses' argument with God reveals a shocking truth to us: Part of the waiting process is giving up our expectations of hearing from God and our desire to work for Him again (Ex. 3:7–7:7).

How Long, O Lord?

When I resigned my pastorate and entered secular work for a season, I had no information from God as to how long this assignment would last or what purposes it would serve. Weeks turned to months and months turned to years as I labored on the night shift of unfulfilled desires, financial stress, and confusion. Why were no doors opening for me? What had I done to merit such divine punishment? Would I ever receive God's permission to return to what I do best?

Following is the wonderful text that focuses on this theme:

How long, O LORD? Will you forget me forever? How long will You hide Your face from me? How long shall I take counsel in my soul, having sorrow in my heart daily? How long will my enemy be exalted over me? (Ps. 13:1–2).

We can sense David's pain as he captures the sentiments of innumerable saints who have stared at God's mantel, watched

61

His timepiece, heard the ticking of the movement, and wondered why the hands moved so s-l-o-w-l-y. The logical conclusion one draws when observing God's apparent inactivity is that He has forgotten, is impotent to help, or simply doesn't care.

I count myself among those who fail to understand how God views time. As I rush through life, worrying about the swift passing of the hours, God is investing long periods of time in preparing His children for comparatively short stints of service. The rhythmic tempo of the heavenly timepiece does not correlate with our earthly clocks and watches.

It is this methodical, plodding God who sometimes allows little children to be taken from godly parents and brought to heaven prematurely. At times this same God leaves the bitter and miserable to live a full life. He takes godly adults in their prime and removes them from their loved ones. He allows impaired children to be born, permits Alzheimer's disease to ravage the mind, and tolerates indescribable misery.

Charley Hanshew was one whose life ended early and abruptly. A seminary student and my dorm R.A. in college, Charley was a godly man who anticipated a lifetime of service for the Savior. After graduation from seminary, he served on the faculty of his alma mater for a few years before fulfilling a dream by returning to his hometown of Martinsburg, West Virginia, to pastor the church that he attended as a child.

Charley's family and ministry were thriving, with two young sons and a strong marriage to his wife, Gracie, when he was struck down. While he was driving through town one day, a construction vehicle rounded a curve, and a heavy piece of equipment fell on Charley's car, killing him instantly.

It is only the divine viewpoint that can make sense out of such a "tragedy." Most who read these words can tell an equally devastating and perplexing tale. In God's timing, Charley Hanshew's flourishing vineyard ministry ended and Charley went into Retirement, leaving his wife and two sons to enter the darkness. A sovereign God determined that it should be so. End of debate.

Though we fail to comprehend His sense of timing, this knowledge of God's ways can still encourage the elderly, the terminally ill, the mentally impaired, and all of those who live or work with the disabled. The closing years of life can naturally become a pit experience. How typical it is for the aging to view their "twilight years" as bereft of meaning. The elderly can easily think that the young, with superior energy, good health, and clearer minds, are "on the cutting edge" while they themselves are "on the shelf." They are tempted to doubt whether their lives have made a difference or if they have value any longer.

But God views the aged, the weak, the infirm, the disabled, the mentally impaired, and the dying—all of these—much differently. Negative thoughts based on our impaired condition must certainly sadden God, who sees everything through a different lens. Such narrow thinking does not allow for His sweeping work in all people of all ages and all conditions as He sovereignly disregards time to achieve His unique purposes in and through each of His children. What a mighty God!

My thoughts were beginning to settle into a "Mosaic" pattern after several months on the night shift, as indicated by my journal:

> Sept. 25, 1992. What am I going to do? Like Moses, I am content caring for "sheep" on the backside of the desert. I have a sort of vision but am not leaving the desert without a burning bush, without an Aaron, without the voice of God urging me. I get up, go to work, come home, eat supper, putter around the house, and go to bed. I have no energy, burden, vision, or sense of calling that drives me beyond this. I don't feel guilty at all because I don't see any other option, but I'm not content to do this indefinitely, either.

Just twelve months after penning these words, I would be called to be the senior pastor of a wonderful body of believers. However, I was unaware of that pending change, for God was not talking to me. For the moment, the darkness was doing its work, causing me to relinquish my dreams and reconcile myself to my "fate." Formerly driven by a vision to lead and shepherd the Body of Christ, I was being forced to let that vision die so that I could get on with the rest of my life. Like Moses, I longed for a life of anonymity in my Midian.

In retrospect, I am startled to see how my night shift experience paralleled Moses' wilderness abyss. It was in his failures that God began tutoring him in the finer nuances of ministry and leadership. For forty years, while Moses tended sheep, God was preparing him for his biggest assignment. The mystery of the pit deepens: oblivious to the hand of God, assuming that the vision is gone forever, Moses is rudely awakened to a change of plans. New rosters are being posted on the vineyard bulletin board.

Content to dwell in Midian, Moses sees a bush ablaze. A Voice speaks! The Unpredictable God again does the unexpected. Moses, standing on holy ground, checks the bulletin board and finds his name moved to the day shift roster. One who has seen his vision crushed by the Divine Hand is startled to discover that he must remove his sandals, for it is always holy ground where God is speaking. Moses' quitting point is actually God's starting line.

Insurrection in the Vineyard

In light of this principle of divine timing, how sad it is to see many believers succumbing to the attractive but bogus teaching that instructs believers to ask God for anything and then to expect (demand) the desired answer. The wrongness of this concept is seen in its unbalanced approach to the biblical teaching concerning prayer. While it is true that the believer is invited to ask much of God (Matt. 7:7-11), we are also instructed that prayer has boundaries (1 John 5:14-15).

The idea that God needs our help to decide when our sufferings should end is a form of *premature closure*, a failure to recognize the divinely imposed constraints or limits to our prayers. Consequently, when mired in a pit experience, we may be wrongly informed that all we need to do is ask God for deliverance, and we can have immediate release. In fact, so goes this dangerous dogma, God is *obligated* to do what we ask Him to do.

Sadly, believers are (unintentionally) misled in their hour of greatest need. The great weakness of this doctrine is the assumption that we are wise enough to understand the best timing for our release from the night shift. To expect God to comply with every request we make takes the duty of making night shift assignments out of the hands of an all-wise God and puts it in the hands of foolish and immature people who rarely know what is best. In fact, taken to its logical conclusion, this erroneous approach to the Christian life encourages us to ask God to spare us from all night shift experiences. If our request were offered in faith, God would be obligated to do so! Of course, there would naturally be no one left to work the night shift in the vineyard. And unhappily, the valuable lessons that are taught only in Night School would go unlearned.

In truth, the Bible's teaching on the value of affliction for the believer is shredded by this shallow approach to prayer and its tragic misunderstanding of how God works in our lives. How many blessings I would have missed if God had actually delivered me from my unpleasant experiences when I asked Him to. Some of my requests of God have been so petulantly childish that I would be embarrassed to reveal them. Like a wise earthly father who refuses a little child's request to play with a sharp knife or run through traffic, God lovingly ignores many of our small-minded demands for release from affliction because He has better things in store for us.

Additionally, it is profoundly arrogant to suggest that a Sovereign God needs us to tell Him when to bring our pit experiences to a close. If God allows the pit, and if He knows what's best for us, why would we presume to tell God when to release us? We dare not put man in the center of the critical decisions that pertain to our training. We must never forget that God is the Teacher and we are the pupils. He is the Father and we are the children. Released prematurely from the night shift, we would be deprived of the benefit of divinely approved affliction.

Much farming takes place in plain view. Wheat, corn, peas, and grapes, for example, all grow in the light of the sun, where progress can be observed. But many of the foods we enjoy result from work done underground. Radishes, potatoes, turnips, carrots, and peanuts, for instance, all grow out of sight. It takes sixty days to grow a radish! Think of it! In the dark soil, hidden from view, the lowly radish grows for two months. Such food would be ruined if the farmer sought to cultivate it on top of the soil.

The Master Farmer knows exactly what is taking place, whether in the light or out of sight.

Why Wait?

Relinquishment is the surrendering of all ambition, dreams, and goals to the authority of Jesus Christ to be consumed as He sees fit. This is the great passion of God for His people and the majestic goal of the pit: that we would love Him with all of our heart, soul, mind, and strength. And time is usually required for us to be ready to relinquish all to Jesus.

Night shift workers learn to worship at a crossroads where the signs point in opposite directions. One sign pointing to mountainous terrain says, "Renounce all personal plans and desires in submission to the will of God." The other sign directs us to lush lowlands and says, "Cling to your rights, possessions, and reputation." While the choice of relinquishment does not end the process, it is clear that the journey cannot proceed without such a decision.

Moses had clearly "relinquished" his vision for emancipating his people from Egypt, and Jeremiah had to relinquish all to God before he could fulfill his miserable, but crucial, vocation. For each, the night shift brought him to the end of his own ambitions and dreams. Whether by choice (as with Jesus), by attrition (as with Moses), or by compulsion (as with Jeremiah), relinquishment becomes the great achievement of the pit. Consciously submitting to God proves that our waiting on Him is productive.

My good friend Joe Ehrmann is a former NFL All-Pro defensive tackle who starred with the Baltimore Colts. Now in retirement, a committed believer, and active in urban ministry and racial reconciliation in the city of Baltimore, Joe is suffering from the after-effects of a violent career. Because of football injuries, Joe's right hip has had to be replaced. This experience was difficult for one who prided himself on resilience, playing through pain, and independence.

After Joe's hip replacement, he walked out onto his porch one winter morning to retrieve the daily newspaper. Stepping on an icy patch, Joe went flying, breaking the femur in his bad leg and damaging his new artificial hip. For months Joe was on crutches as he waited for the doctors to determine what to do about his predicament.

After about five months in this personalized pit, Joe was asked to share his experience with a small group of men. The air was heavy with intensity as he related the work of God in his life, using two crutches to break him of his pride, his self-will, and his independent spirit. A fall on a porch on a winter day set in motion an internal work in the heart of a former football player. Such a God-sized project is more astounding than anything Joe ever encountered while wearing pads and helmet.

When we play on God's gridiron, it's not two-hand touch played delicately by nice guys. Human football is child's play compared with God's cross-body blocks as we are weaned from self. Lovingly blindsided under cover of darkness, we are stunned by bone-jarring, heart-crunching tackles designed to break our will and our heart.

Since that first hip replacement and his fall, Joe has had a second hip replacement to correct the damage. Those who believe that the children of God are not to suffer might rebuke Joe for his unbelief. "Just ask God to heal your hip and throw those crutches away!" would be a predictable recommendation. To such a comment, I suspect Joe's response might be something like: "I wouldn't think of trading what God is doing in my life for my original, healthy hip. The pain has been worth it, for God is working deep inside of me where no one can see, touching the diseases of my heart and soul. No, thank you! In spite of all of the misery, I'll let the pit have its perfect work in my life."

The End Explains

God stretches Israel's journey from Sinai to Canaan into a forty-year trek. And Moses spends eighty long years in preparation for forty years of leadership. By divine appointment, I spent thirty excruciatingly long months laboring at a distasteful assignment. The timetable of our patient God certainly differs from ours, doesn't it?

The length of the wait is not as significant as its intensity. There is a natural human consequence when daylight fades. Scientific studies on the effect of light deprivation on human behavior indicate that humans become disoriented when denied access to sunlight and moonlight. In such situations, one's biological clock resets itself to a schedule other than the normal twenty-four-hour day. Individuals kept in solitary confinement or subjected to extreme pain and torture testify that their sense of time became greatly distorted.

The story of Christian martyrs supports this point. When one suffers intensely under cover of darkness, time seems to be suspended. The sufferer is disoriented as to the passing of hours and days. God's people wait for different lengths of time, but the wait always seems long when one is in the darkness.

In January of 1956, it was exceptionally difficult to comprehend the divine intent for Jim Elliot and four other godly young men slain in Ecuador. Notice the heavenly timetable:

February 1952—Jim Elliot sails for Ecuador.

October 1953—Jim and Elisabeth Elliot are married in Ecuador.

January 1956—Auca Indians kill Jim and four other men.

Five young men, full of promise, hearts set on reaching lost Indians with the Gospel of Jesus Christ, were taken into eternity before they could barely begin their work.

Who can fathom the Mind behind such decisions? These men began Retirement while five wives and several small children started their lengthy night shift assignments. We are face-to-face with the hidden wisdom of God. One can only bow in the presence of a God whose time schedule operates like this.

When we see the Master Planner in Glory, we will be enjoying Retirement from our vineyard labors. At that time, any unanswered questions about the night shift can be posed to our Sovereign Lord. The reasoning behind His decisions will become apparent, the "secret formula" for night shift assignments will be revealed, and we will worship God for His incredible love and marvelous wisdom. If we ask, "Sovereign God, why did You take the lives of five young husbands and fathers while they were in their prime?" the answer will astound us and we will kneel in adoration.

In the inimitable words of Amy Carmichael, "the end" will all make sense:

The crossed endeavor, earnest purpose foiled,

The strange bewilderment of good work spoiled,

The clinging weariness, the inward strain?

Will not the End explain?

Meanwhile He comforteth

Them that are losing patience; 'tis His way

But none can write the words they hear Him say,

For men to read, only they know He saith

Kind words, and comforteth.

Not that He doth explain

The mystery that baffleth; but in a sense

Husheth the quiet heart, that far, far hence

Lieth a field set thick with golden grain,

Wetted in seedling days by many a rain.

The End, it will explain.[1]

---

[1] "The End Will Explain" found in

Judith Couchman, ed. *A Very Present Help* (Ann Arbor, Mich.: Servant Publications, 1996), p. 159.

Frank Houghton, *Amy Carmichael of Dohnavur: The Story of a Lover and Her Beloved* (London: S.P.C.K., 1953), p. 72.

The more we contemplate the lives of godly people, whether in the Bible or in the history of the Church, we are confronted with a consistent truth: The night shift is for every believer, and God's timetable for His children is never what we think it should be.

Moses, the abject failure, the lowly shepherd in Midian, became a mighty instrument in God's hand because he had to wait. The waiting bore great fruit in his life, as is always the case for those who allow God to do His work in His timing and in His way.

Waiting in the pit, we cry incessantly to God for our release. Fervent prayer becomes the great lesson of affliction. David certainly learned that lesson well when he found his name on the night shift roster. . . .

* * *

The waiter's prayer:

Dear Lord, it seems to take so long for You to do something about the predicaments of my life. I wait and wait and nothing seems to happen. At times I feel like giving up. Teach me to wait for You to work, not giving You a deadline or demanding that You do things my way. I realize that Your timetable is different from mine and that You will do the right thing in my life at the right time. I pray this in the name of Jesus, Amen.

Give ear to my words, O LORD,

consider my groaning.

Heed the sound of my cry for help,

my King and my God,

for to You I pray.

Psalm 5:1–2

STAGE THREE
THE CRY

David and the Cave
(1 Sam. 24:1–22)

The barren western coast of the Dead Sea became David's base of operations. Unlike Saul, who was from the tribe of Benjamin, David could find his way easily across the stark Judean landscape. Not far from his home of Bethlehem, this was familiar territory for the former shepherd. He had tended his flocks in this area on many occasions, and now, constantly on the run, he moved comfortably among the rocks and caves of the wilderness near Engedi.

So it was that David and some of his men took refuge in one of the many caves overlooking the sea. Seeking rest in the coolness at the rear of the cavern, the weary fugitives shared some of their meager store of bread and wine and tried to get some sleep. Their plan called for them to wait until nightfall before moving to a new location.

While the other men napped or talked quietly in small groups, David and Joab huddled next to a large boulder as they traced in the dirt a possible route. "Shhh!"

73

At the sound, David jerked his head around instinctively. Abishai, Joab's brother and David's nephew, held his finger to his lips. As one of David's security guards, Abishai had been guarding the entrance to the cave. The clamor of voices outside brought him to full alert as the men scrambled for their weapons. Abishai crawled to the very mouth of the cave to investigate and returned quickly, his eyes wide with alarm. "It's Saul and about five units of soldiers!" he whispered hoarsely.

David was stunned. Of all the caves in this wilderness area, why had Saul picked this one? From the sounds of laughter and bantering nearby, David knew that the king was unaware that his prey was holed up inside.

Beads of sweat broke out on David's forehead. What could they do? Outnumbered by superior forces, they were trapped and doomed if Saul detected their presence. Life had been such a strain for David, living on the run, staying just one step ahead of his pursuers. Now King Saul chose this very spot for a visit.

His stomach tied in knots, David motioned his men further back into the dark recesses, hoping that the contingent of soldiers would pass by. Huddled in the darkness, David stifled his gasp as a tall, solitary figure wandered in. It was Saul, and he was alone.

Pausing just inside the entrance, Saul took off his robe and threw it on a pile of rocks in David's direction. It was obvious that the king was preparing to relieve himself.

"Now's your chance," one of David's men whispered. "He's vulnerable. Go get him!"

Stealthily making his way toward Saul, David reached for the robe that the king had nonchalantly tossed aside. The noisy shuffling of mules and men just outside the cave made it easy for him to avoid detection. With knife in hand, he cut a piece from the robe and crept back to his hiding place, motioning his men to be still until the king left the cave.

Although his companions pleaded for permission to kill Saul, David's heart was smitten with conviction. When the royal search party moved just a short distance away, David came to the mouth of the cave and shouted to Saul, "My lord, the king!" Startled, Saul turned to see who was calling.

Bowing respectfully, David shouted, "Why do you want to harm me? You can see by this piece that I cut from your robe that I could have killed you in the cave if I had wished."

Saul gaped at David, remembering the young boy who had slain Goliath. He recalled the countless hours David had spent soothing Saul's spirit with his special musical gifts. Now it was a young warrior, tired, dirty, and perturbed, who confronted the king.

It was a rare moment of honest introspection for Saul. Seeing David's decency in the face of his own treachery, the truth hit home. Ashamed of himself and weeping, Saul slowly turned around and quietly dismissed his troops.

After watching Saul's militia ride off, David returned to the cave. The ragtag band of mercenaries and friends gathered around him, pounding his back in jubilation over their narrow escape.

But David was strangely subdued. "Let me have a little time to myself, men," he said as he took some writing materials out of his leather knapsack. Moving behind a large rock, he sat down and began to scratch out the words to a song:

Be gracious to me, O God, be gracious to me, for my soul takes refuge in You; and in the shadow of Your wings I will take refuge until destruction passes by. I will cry to God Most High, to God who accomplishes all things for me. He will send from heaven and save me; He reproaches him who tramples upon me (Ps. 57:1-3).

The heading of Psalm 57 ("A Mikhtam of David, when he fled from Saul in the cave") indicates that David penned this psalm after the encounter with Saul recorded in 1 Samuel 24. In that incident, David learned the priceless lesson of Stage Three— "He . . . heard my cry" (Ps. 40:1). Yes, the pit is the place where prayer is best learned.

God's Prayer Classroom

On the night shift, once-smug and self-satisfied individuals see their facades of independence and self-reliance crumble. True weaknesses and needs are uncovered. A cry of desperation is the result of this ruthless disclosure. This shift accomplishes its purpose when it produces serious people who, with great urgency, cry out to God.

When my oldest son, Danny, was born, he had a little quiver in his lower lip that displayed itself when he began to cry. Each time some mysterious need presented itself, he demanded instantaneous resolution. If his need was not met immediately, the quiver developed larger dimensions while his face took on a reddish hue. As his features became contorted, his vocal cords increased their output in quantum surges. Indignant that the big people who always hovered over him had failed to promptly dispatch the appropriate remedy, Danny would screech at full volume. His ultimatum came when, intent upon presenting his case with facial contortions and loud protestations, he neglected to draw air into his lungs. The sounds ceased, his little eyes filled with tears, his face reddened, and his tiny fists clenched in fury. This was one desperate baby.

David, the psalmist, understands this kind of desperation. A valuable lesson in prayer is one benefit of time spent on the night shift. Deprived of what they feel is rightfully theirs, angry that the Owner has given them the short end of the stick, night shift employees lift their voices in a chorus of indignation. They know what they want, and they have decided to cry out for justice.

Cry Principles

Out of this milieu of trauma, despair, and frustration, the Word of God offers us five "Cry Principles" to encourage night shift laborers to talk to their God:

CRY PRINCIPLE #1: *Desperate circumstances produce prayerful people.* The impact of the pit is seen in David's cry to God, for how many of us would pray earnestly, fervently, and consistently if we were not frantically hanging on for dear life?

As I labored in the dark, I observed, in retrospect, that the seasons of greatest calm also were the times when I prayed least. How different was my prayer life during times of stress and difficulty! Frequently, as a pastor, with church troubles inundating me, I would shout to God for help. This cry did not usually come after I preached a particularly good sermon, but when things seemed to be falling apart. Later, while driving the streets of Baltimore carrying my daily load of heating oil, I found myself pleading with God for relief!

October 1, 1992. Prayer is growing in its meaning and significance for me. No, I am not a prayer warrior, by any means. But my present work and schedule allows for "praying without ceasing." I wish I could master that concept.

Admittedly, the rest of these prayers were very selfish as I focused on my problems. But regardless of content, I was crying out to God, and that is prayer. I knew that my Heavenly Father was delighted to hear my voice under any circumstances.

CRY PRINCIPLE #2: *The darkness produces brokenness, and broken people pray fervently.* There is a marked difference between the prayer of the self-righteous and that of the humble person. While Luke 18:9-14 clearly makes the point that both types of people pray, there is a vast contrast between the prayer that stems from self-confidence and the desperate cry flowing from the heart of the one working on the night shift.

The night shift is able to produce a "broken and contrite spirit" in us because:

1. We understand that we cannot now, of our own free will, leave the pit.

2. In the darkness we are shocked to discover that, on the day shift, our productivity in the vineyard was far less than we imagined.

3. The darkness compels us to confront and evaluate the reasons for our lack of productivity.

4. Former self-reliance and pride are exposed and we realize that, in our helpless condition, we must depend on Another.

5. Any facade of capability, success, or maturity crumbles, and we come to see ourselves as pathetically weak.

6. Our tight grip on things formerly esteemed as important is forcibly loosened, and we are given a new set of vineyard values.

7. We can now perceive that our future will necessitate an ongoing condition of spiritual poverty.

8. We acknowledge our sin and God's holiness and are brought to our knees as the pit provides a laboratory for self- and God-discovery.

For the sojourner in the pit, defeat and failure are the precursors to brokenness. In failing to reach our goal, we become shattered people. Brokenness, a priceless commodity in the economy of God, is the accepted legal tender of the night shift. It is the gold and silver of the vineyard, the currency carried in the wallets of those who have gone to Night School and learned their lessons well. Flowing freely from the Son to each night shift worker and returning to the Owner, this precious quality of brokenness stabilizes the resources of the vineyard and makes the vineyard productive.

Evaluating vineyard output in these terms naturally raises the question, *Just exactly what is success and failure in vineyard productivity?* It is biblically axiomatic that what we humanly perceive to be failure may, in reality, often be a time of great progress. The era of those nineteen post-seminary years—when I saw my lack of productivity become apparent—was a painful season of my ministry. Leaving seminary with solid theology, enthusiasm, dreams, and spiritual giftedness—without a clue as to the nature of true success, but convinced I could not fail—I ultimately sought to identify the reason for my ministerial malaise. With all of my good theology, why did it take me so long to discover that the problem was *me*?

How easily we may succumb to the appeal of attributing intrinsic value to attendance, funds, buildings, large staffs, and a wide following. When those "success indicators" are missing or fail us, we are left to scratch our heads and ponder our failure.

Assessing these fickle and fragile proofs as signs of success may necessitate a semester or so in Night School to learn the Owner's standards of true achievement. For me, a sovereign God was lovingly breaking me of my pride and self-confidence. I now view that protracted season of barrenness and brokenness as a time when God began a deep work in my heart.

We are tempted to blame our perceived lack of accomplishment on external tokens—the difficult people we serve, lack of funds, the company for which we work, a poor supervisor, the climate in which we are forced to labor, or even Satan. In reality, if God is sovereign over those people and circumstances, and He is, we are left with God and God alone. David prospered in spite of Saul and his minions. There is no need to blame others. Our lack of productivity is a God-driven blessing intended to reveal something in us that needs repair. When true brokenness occurs, blaming subsides, and we are able to embrace "failure" and kneel before God with the prayer of the broken heart of Moses (Ex. 32:13, 18).

This is undoubtedly the intent of Acts 2:41–47, Hebrews 10:25, and other similar passages, which exhort the Body of Christ to assemble. No perfunctory gathering to punch our spiritual time cards for another week, the meetings of Jesus' Body are desperate rallies intended to compel wretched human failures (pastors included!) to kneel at the foot of the cross *together*. Composed of the helpless, weak, foolish, and contrite, this Church convenes in brokenness, seeking the grace of God on display in the lives of other brothers and sisters who themselves are dependent on God's mercy. In such a climate of surrender and spiritual poverty, encouragement is assured while the pit is being endured.

To all pastors, Christian workers, and believers in general who are despairing over their *apparent* lack of success in ministry, I offer some simple advice. True achievement in ministry burgeons when failure is embraced and God is allowed to place us on the night shift of His vineyard, where we will labor in the "Department of Defeat." His grand design is to bring proud, independent disciples to a point of prayerful surrender so that they will learn to lean on Him for their strength.

On the streets of Baltimore, I wore the clothes of the working man: a nice blue uniform with the insignia of the company that sent me out each day in a shiny truck to deliver fifty-four hundred gallons of heating oil. Steel-toed work shoes protected my feet. My hands were no longer the clean, soft hands of a white-collar cleric, for I could never completely remove all of the grime after a day's work.

I noticed that my prayers were transformed along with my appearance. My conversations with God had moved from the antiseptic, sanctified utterances of a theoretician who was comfortable in his piety. Now passionate, earthy cries—yes, even screams for survival—burst forth from my altered vocal cords. But whether as a laborer driving a truck or as a pastor of a church, brokenness was produced in me as the night shift suspended all sense of achievement so that I would become more desperate. Thanks to the night shift, I became a blue-collar pray-er.

CRY PRINCIPLE #3: *True prayer in the pit includes complaining*. During my time on the night shift, I found myself broadsided with this theme from the Psalms. Psalm 40, in particular, piqued my curiosity on the subject, so I began to investigate.

I was astonished to discover that more than 15 percent of the content of Psalms can be construed as complaint. That's a rather high percentage for a section of the Bible we generally view as emphasizing praise and worship.

This discovery raised a question in my blue-collar brain: If the psalmist is comfortable complaining, why aren't most believers at ease with it? Perhaps our approach to music in worship is symptomatic of our avoidance of the doctrine of biblical complaining. While we enjoy a wealth of praise choruses and hymns drawn directly from the Psalms, where are the "complaint choruses" in our worship services? After all, should not our fellowship in worship include the dimensions of the spiritual walk that are common to all? Perhaps unbelievers and the afflicted would find more "reality" in our worship were we able to focus on our shared experience as strangers "in a dry and weary land where there is no water" (Ps. 63:1).

Don't be mistaken: this is not fleshly introspection but the pathway to greater worship. Biblical worship is most glorifying to God and meaningful to us when it affirms the authenticity of our hardship and extols the magnificence of the Savior, who "was despised and forsaken of men, a man of sorrows and acquainted with grief" (Isa. 53:3).

Musing on this question, I concluded that our view of worship does not easily factor in the authentic struggles of walking with God. We naturally focus on that which we believe is more uplifting. We don't sing about the darkness and about God forgetting us because it doesn't suit our theology, our emotions, or our preferences.

Two simple conclusions emerged from my unscientific "research." First, we are not very comfortable talking to God as the psalmist did. Second, if our worship is to be authentic biblical adoration, it should include complaint and honest dialogue with God.

CRY PRINCIPLE #4: *Biblical complaining is worship.* After analyzing prayer-complaint, I concluded that protesting to God could actually be a declaration of worship. Look at it this way:

A. If I thought that God had no control over the pit experiences that have come my way, I wouldn't even be taking the time to protest to Him.

B. If God couldn't manage the future outcome of my current night shift assignment, I would have no reason to be complaining to Him.

C. Therefore, by complaining directly to God, I am acknowledging His sovereignty over my past, present, and future night shift experiences. This is worship.

Another way of recognizing complaining as worship is to note the kind of terminology the psalmist often uses in his arguments with God. Most of these complaints fall into one of ten categories. Check and see how many of these categories describe the desperation of your prayer life:

1. God's wake-up call: "Arouse Yourself for me; You have appointed judgment.... Stir up Yourself, and awake to my right and to my cause, my God and my Lord.... Arouse Yourself, why do You sleep, O Lord?" (Ps. 7:6; 35:23; 44:23). *Hmmm ... the way things are going for me, God must be taking a nap.*

2. God's motivational call: "Arise, O Lord, do not let man prevail.... Arise, O Lord; O God, lift up Your hand.... Do not forget the humble. Let God arise, let His enemies be scattered.... Rise up, O Judge of the earth" (Ps. 9:19; 10:12; 68:1; 94:2). *Maybe I can get God moving.*

3. A divine all-points bulletin: "You, O Lord, be not far off.... My eyes fail while I wait for my God.... O God of hosts, turn again now, we beseech You" (Ps. 22:19; 69:3; 80:14). *Now where is God? He was just here a little while ago.*

4. A double-check of God's timing: "How long, O Lord? Will You forget me forever? How long will You hide your face from me? ... How long, O Lord? Will You be angry forever? ... O Lord God of hosts, how long will You be angry with the prayer of Your people? ... Do return, O Lord; how long will it be?" (Ps. 13:1; 79:5; 80:4; 90:13). *It sure is taking God an awfully long time to do whatever it is He's doing!*

5. Clarification of God's intent: "Why do You stand afar off, O Lord? Why do You hide Yourself in times of trouble? ... O God, why have You rejected us forever? Why does Your anger smoke against the sheep of your pasture?" (Ps. 10:1; 74:1). *I wonder what God is really up to, what with all of these problems I'm having.*

6. Moving God into high gear: "O God, hasten to deliver me; O Lord, hasten to my help! ... In the day when I call, answer me quickly" (Ps. 70:1; 102:2). *If I hint and nag, maybe God will pick up the pace.*

7. The not-so-subtle reminder: "You are He who brought me forth from the womb; You made me trust when upon my mother's breasts.... You have been my God from my mother's womb. Be not far from me, for trouble is near; for there is none to help.... None of those who wait for You will be ashamed" (Ps. 22:9-11; 25:3). *Lord, remember me? Didn't You commit Yourself to me? Aren't You obligated not to forget me?*

8. A fear that God has changed and become irresponsible: "Will He never be favorable again? Has His lovingkindness ceased forever? Has His promise come to an end forever? Has God forgotten to be gracious?" (Ps. 77:7-9). *God used to be so reliable, but lately He doesn't seem to be treating me right.*

9. *Deus Absconditus:* "My God, my God, why have You forsaken me? Far from my deliverance are the words of my groaning.... O God, do not remain quiet; do not be silent and, O God, do not be still.... I have called upon You every day, O LORD.... Do not hide Your face from me in the day of my distress.... O God of my praise, do not be silent!" (Ps. 22:1; 83:1; 88:9; 102:2; 109:1). *I feel abandoned by You, God! Why would You leave me now?*

10. Generic grumbling, also known as "dumping on God": "I am reckoned among those who go down to the pit; I have become like a man without strength, forsaken among the dead, like the slain who lie in the grave, whom You remember no more, and they are cut off from Your hand. You have put me in the lowest pit, in dark places, in the depths. Your wrath has rested upon me, and You have afflicted me with all Your waves.... For the enemy has persecuted my soul; he has crushed my life to the ground. He has made me dwell in dark places, like those who have long been dead. Therefore my spirit is overwhelmed within me; my heart is appalled within me" (Ps. 88:4-7; 143:3-4). *God, I'm sick of this mess and I don't mind telling You so, either!*

These references from the Psalms highlight the doubts and dissatisfaction we may experience as we view God's treatment of His children. Strangely, these same words also acknowledge His power, for such thoughts assume that, although the petitioner does not have the answer, God does. As a little child's inquiries imply that Mommy and Daddy are smarter and stronger, so raising questions with God is an admission of our own limitations while simultaneously attributing greatness to Him.

Common among God's children is the need to express outrage over perceived injustice and God's apparent indifference in the night seasons of life. Over a period of time, these emotions build up and must be vented. The fifth Cry Principle anticipates precisely such needs.

CRY PRINCIPLE #5: *Night shift prayer-complaining is usually an expression of anger at God.* The psalmist never apologizes to God for complaining. He talks to God as if he's unconcerned with the possibility of hurting His feelings or making Him angry. He even sometimes hints that God is to blame for his problems. David is annoyed, frustrated, and disillusioned—and makes no bones about it! To our surprise, God seems able to take it. Apparently His feelings don't get wounded as easily as ours.

From our twenty-first century, sophisticated perspective, such dialogue with the Almighty seems somehow rude or discourteous. When I speak of this principle, I see the furrowed brows of those who think such God-talk borders on the blasphemous. Reluctant to tell God what we *really* think, we shrink back from actually blaming Him lest we show Him disrespect. However, when we fail to speak honestly, we are not really communicating with the Almighty. And, if God is sovereign, truthful communication may require that we tell Him that *it is His fault!* Certainly our Old Testament counterparts felt free to do so (Ps. 39:10; 77:3; 118:18; Lam. 2:20).

* * *

Moses felt he was at the breaking point. How much more of these people's complaints could he take? If it wasn't a lack of water, then it was the menu, or their circuitous route, or his leadership style. The list of grievances was endless. Murmur and gripe, murmur and gripe.

This time it was the manna. Who knew what they would find to grouse about tomorrow? This motley Israelite crew always craved something else. How about a little variety in the menu? Roast beef, veal, lamb, leeks, onions, desert hare, asp, garlic—anything but manna.

Moses could hear them in their tents. He tired of listening to their daily litany of woes. "Man, I'm so sick of this stuff I'm ready to gag. If I see one more piece of manna, I'll throw it right in Aaron's face."

"Yeah, Moses deserves some payback, too," another observed. "It was his idea to take us to Canaan. If you've never led a large group through the desert, why not admit it and go get some help?"

Finally Moses, having taken all of the abuse he could handle, felt the blood rush to his face. Both angry and afraid, he hurried to the tabernacle and prostrated himself before the Lord. Stretching his arms before him, he blurted out, "God, why are You treating me like this? I've tried to serve You faithfully and all You do is dump the burdens of leadership on me. I didn't conceive these people, that I should have the responsibility for their care. And where could I possibly get food for all of them? This is too much for one man to bear! The load is too great. So, just kill me. Right here and now. Do me in and let's get it over with."

In one episode (Num. 11:1–35), Moses released all of the frustrations and anxieties that had been bottled up inside.

How to Talk with God

While we admire Moses for his authentic dialogue with God, we may not feel comfortable with this kind of honesty. But is not this type of human-to-divine exchange the sort of interaction good parents love to have with their children: forthright, controlled, honest, respectful?

What responsible parent doesn't take great delight in a lively exchange of ideas with his child? We all know how a typical conversation might go: "Son, how was school today? Learn anything new?" This probing question, posed to a teenager chewing on a cookie, may elicit the profound response, "Grbmkfl," as chocolate milk drips off the chin.

How much better if the child were to initiate the conversation with something like, "Uh, Dad, I've been doing some thinking. Things haven't been going too well around here lately. I'm pretty unhappy with the rules you've made up. And my allowance . . . well . . . give me a break! What do you say, Dad? Can we talk about it?"

This teenager may be complaining, but at least he is dialoguing respectfully with his parent. Two-way verbal interaction, even if it involves criticism, brings great delight to the Lord, for He is a Father who loves to communicate with His children.

The heavenly communication lines were open for Moses and David and all the other great complainers in Scripture. It seems that God allows this kind of kind of frank talk and probably even welcomes it. Surely He longs for His children to confess their true feelings about their night shift assignments. This is, in fact, part of the mystique of the darkness, for we have seen that the complaint of the night worker is, "God won't speak to me!" In reality, the afflicted one eventually discovers that God is just waiting for him to initiate the conversation. True, we may begin communicating with God out of our anger and frustration. But at least we are finally conversing with the One who can make a difference, and that's what counts.

* * *

It didn't take me very long on the night shift to discover that I was angry with God. My first post-seminary assignment was as an associate pastor in a lively and growing church. But there was a dark side to some of the relationships. The waters, already murky when I arrived, began to churn in earnest shortly after my appearance on staff. When charges were leveled against the senior pastor, I was thrust into the middle to try to bring reconciliation. Even though this pastor was eventually exonerated of the accusations, the conflict continued.

Aha! My thoughts bordered on conceit. *This is the moment for which I was born.* I was Moses: young, cocky, and ready for any conflict. But unexpectedly I became the object of the assault. As combat heated up, I managed to kill a few "Egyptians," bury some bodies in the sand, and win a few skirmishes.

However, eighteen months later, defeated and discouraged, I resigned my post, fleeing Egypt for Midian. I was battered, bruised, broken, and very, very angry. The war had been lost. What started out as a well-intentioned attempt on my part to bring reconciliation between estranged parties ended with my being falsely accused by the very ones I was trying to help.

Oh, how very wrong I was in my misdirected rage. Eventually I came to understand that I was actually angry with God. The events that wounded me so acutely were, in reality, a part of the sovereignty of God in my life. Although God could have prevented those painful circumstances, He instead granted them access to my life. I was mad at God and resented His assigning me to the night shift, yet I inadvertently devised a strategy designed to take it out on His human instruments when I should have been complaining to Him.

It doesn't take a degree in rocket science for me to look back at my own circumstances as an associate pastor and see the hand of God directing my affairs. I now know that while my Heavenly Father was carefully instructing me in Night School classes, I was responding with anger to the faculty He had appointed to teach me. In fact, I have concluded that almost all anger in the Christian life is directed at God. Oh, we may think we're targeting our spouse, our kids, our boss, the dog, the neighbor, the plugged shower drain, the other driver, or the leaky roof; but if we believe in God's sovereignty, then we must assume that our problems are ultimately His fault. Our anger, therefore, if vented in any direction, should be intended for *Him*.

When I figured this out, I started talking to God like David did, expressing my anger in ways that were honest but respectful. As I did so, I became more focused on God, more oriented to His way of thinking, and less preoccupied with my "enemies." God was my problem, not people. It is He who is in control.

Our Sovereign Lord

The reader now experiencing great trials, perhaps spending an inordinate amount of time on the night shift, may struggle with a cogent view of divine sovereignty. Entering into the deepest of all mysteries, we scratch our heads and ponder the inscrutable wisdom of God. By what "secret formula" are night shift assignments determined?

First, please understand that I am not talking about affliction that comes as a result of God's punishment for sins we commit. Many believers, finding themselves in dire straits, may struggle with guilt from assuming that their difficulties have resulted from their own sin. While it is true that God does discipline us for disobedience (see an account of the built-in consequences of David's sin in 2 Sam. 11), that topic must be reserved for another discussion. Night shift assignments may sometimes be a result of sin, but I am not now writing about the night shift as punishment.

Second, I am not suggesting that God directly *causes* all of the difficulties we encounter while in the pit. Such a view would require the parents of a profoundly disabled child, for example, to conclude: *God caused our child to be impaired,* or for the father of a little girl who has been raped to believe that this heinous act was God's plan. While this view has some advantages and is espoused by various godly theologians, it is biblically acceptable to adopt other ways of looking at such matters. While some Christians prefer the idea that God "ordains" suffering, others believe that the Bible teaches a softer view of providence—that He "allows" affliction. This small volume cannot even begin to address the strengths and weaknesses of each of these perspectives.

Of course, no matter where you pitch your theological tent, God's decision-making process remains shrouded in some degree of mystery. But the biblical view of the sovereignty of God *does not necessarily require* that we see Him as causing that which He hates.

What I am suggesting is that our sovereign Lord has the right and authority to dictate a night shift assignment for any of His children. We know this to be true of God's own Son, who was "the

Lamb slain from the foundation of the world" (Rev. 13:8, NKJV). In order to achieve His larger purposes, God may sometimes ordain or allow specific hardships for any of His children. Should this be the case, it is only for good, since God's love for His children thwarts any exercise that would be injurious to us. All night shift assignments will prove to be for good, whether they were sovereignly decreed, divinely permitted, or simply the consequences of living in a fallen world.

Finally, if you hear me declare that God is so fully and completely sovereign that (a) He has the power to use all circumstances in our lives for good and, (b) He is mighty enough to prevent any circumstance if He so chooses, then you're right on the money. The Father's permission is needed before any trial can afflict His child. All believers, regardless of their systematic theology on the issue of ordination, providence, and predestination, can agree on this one conclusion: *God is constantly at work to guarantee that everything that comes our way will turn out for good.* In fact, He promises this very thing!

Joseph, son of Jacob, reinforces this lesson for all sufferers. Who was betrayed and mistreated by friends and family more than Joseph? His comments to his brothers when he addressed their outrageous treatment of him help us realize our anger and distrust are with God, not with people. Notice what Joseph told his siblings:

> *God sent me* before you to preserve life.... *God sent me* before you to preserve for you a remnant in the earth, and to keep you alive by a great deliverance. Now, therefore, it was not you who sent me here, *but God.... God has made me* lord of Egypt.... As for you, you meant evil against me, but God meant it for good (Gen. 45:5, 7–9; 50:20).

No matter what your circumstance, God means it for good!

Quit Your Bellyachin'!

The pit begins to have a wonderful impact on us when our anger is discovered, analyzed, and transformed into conversation with God. We are now in a position to contemplate the reality of the cry of Psalm 40. "This poor man cried, and the LORD heard him" (Ps. 34:6). No feeble, well-rehearsed, polished prayer, these words! Hardly verbalized in "religious-speak," this earthy exclamation originates from within the pit. This is a "dirt-under-the-fingernails" kind of prayer.

The person who prays this way will not be turned away. He is not interested in phraseology or flowery terms, nor is he attempting to impress with vocabulary or syntax. Like my newborn son and his desperate wails for assistance, this night shift employee will not be denied an audience with the vineyard's Owner.

Biblical invitations to complain, however, carry a word of caution. Our model for proper complaining is the psalmist, not Israel in the wilderness. Biblical prayer-complaint honors God. The difference is important. *Fleshly* complaining is "complaining to others about how God is treating me." *Godly* complaining is "complaining to God about how He is treating me." There are countless examples in Scripture of improper complaining. These case studies provide a warning to us.

God often punished the nation of Israel for what the Bible calls "murmuring." For a good illustration of such grousing, read Exodus 16:1–13 and 17:1–7. Inappropriate complaining (murmuring) stands in contrast to proper complaints in five crucial ways:

1. *Murmurers complain about what God has done*, all the while failing to recognize that it is God's work about which they murmur (Ex. 16:2). Although God is working in their circumstances, they are incapable of tracing His hand in their lives. In contrast, godly complaining properly blames God for what is happening.

2. *Murmurers talk to others.* Those who grumble are really griping about God but are not actually talking to God (Ex. 16:8). In contrast, a godly complaint is reported to Him. While the Hebrews were more likely to whine to others rather than to God, David was rarely found addressing his complaints to people.

3. *Murmurers are captivated by the "hopelessness" of their pit experience,* while biblical complainers know that God is able to deliver (Ex. 17:1-3). Godly protesters call on God to do what they know He can do, whereas murmurers have given up hope.

4. *Murmurers lash out at whatever or whomever is most convenient to blame,* while biblical complainers know that they are angry with God (Ex. 17:4). When anger surfaces in the Psalms, God is on the receiving end. This is noticeably true in the "imprecatory" psalms, where the psalmist calls for the destruction of his enemies. He rails not directly against his foes, but cries to God for their punishment.

5. *Those who murmur can only envision the worst,* while those who complain to God remember His promises and remind Him of His obligations (Ex. 14:10-12). Unbelieving griping is centered on the "worst-case scenario," while godly complaining has God's own Word on the front burner.

As a leader in ministry, I cannot ignore the reality that much complaining in the church is directed at the leaders whom God raised up. Just like Moses and Aaron, modern-day church leaders are flawed people chosen to lead by God's grace. The congregation is in need of seeing the brokenness of its leaders. When church and ministry leaders operate out of their poverty, the sovereign God who has raised up that same leadership can properly deal with the resistance of the flock.

Rebellion against the established leadership of the church, like the resentment of Israel toward Moses' leadership, is tantamount to revolt against God Himself. (The exception, of course, is where obvious and blatant sin exists among the leaders.) How much resistance to church leaders, though often easily justified and rationalized, may ultimately prove to be rebellion against God Himself?

God's people murmured against one another; they griped at Moses and Aaron in utter unbelief. Rather than an articulation of their heartfelt concerns to God, their murmuring was vented to others *about* God. They did not lift their voices in reverence to address their grievances to the Holy One of Israel, nor were they interested in the divine solution to human problems.

Since this lesson of "The Cry" is so essential, God waits patiently until we get the point. He loves the cries of His people and is long-suffering while we learn to pray. Waiting for such a long, long time, we cry, cry, and cry some more. It is then that "The Answer" comes, often when it is least expected and in the most mysterious ways. . . .

A night shift cry:

> *Dear Lord, You know how much I hate the situation I'm in right now. But You have permitted these events to come my way and so I come to You for help, crying out for release from this night shift assignment. All of my trust and hope is in You. If You do not deliver me, I have nowhere else to turn. I wait for You to answer this prayer in the best way and at the best time. Amen.*

Blessed is the man

whom You chasten, O Lord,

and whom You teach out of Your law.

Psalm 94:12

It is good for me that I was afflicted,

that I may learn Your statutes.

Psalm 119:71

The word of God came to John,

the son of Zacharias,

in the wilderness.

Luke 3:2

STAGE FOUR
THE ANSWER

John and the Word of God
(Luke 1:1–3:6)

John sat in the mouth of the cave that he currently called home, his back propped against a boulder. Here he could recline in the shade and look across the valley through the haze of the oppressive midday heat. Today's lunch had been especially tasteless. Chewing the last bite of his meager noontime meal, John prepared for a brief nap.

Sound sleep eluded him. Something stirred inside of him, a yearning that he had not yet figured out. Restless and deep in thought, he stretched, rose, and strolled down to the tiny spring that supplied his drinking water.

With a desire to confront others with the things he had been learning about Jehovah's holiness, John was considering leaving the desert to preach. His understanding of the coming of the Messiah had matured with his recent readings, particularly in the Isaiah scrolls he had been able to collect. Sipping the cool spring water, John contemplated his conviction that this One was coming soon. Isaiah had indicated that a unique person would prepare the way for Him to be received. *What an honor it would be,* John mused, *to prepare Messiah's way.*

Wandering up to a ridge that offered a view of the Judean wilderness, John could see shepherds tending their flocks in the distance. Most of the citizenry in the region of Engedi recognized John as a recluse and avoided him. Only a handful of people in this area had ever heard John talk or seen him in the company of others. Appearing to dislike people, to be one of those "crazies" in every small town, he gave them plenty of reasons to ignore him. John, of course, preferred it that way.

How could I ever explain this calling I've had on my life? he thought, reflecting over thirty years of wilderness existence. If he couldn't explain his strange life, how could anyone else possibly understand?

John knew he had come to a keener understanding of God's ways during these decades of asceticism. Living alone, away from society, he had become acquainted with the God of Abraham in a way that few could appreciate. With little else to do beyond his study and the daily tasks needed for survival—washing, acquiring food, cooking, sleeping—John was able to spend considerable time studying the Torah. Developing a deep love for the law of God, he committed enormous portions of the Mosaic and prophetic scrolls to memory.

Returning to his cave, John pulled out his collection of scrolls. In the last five or six years, he found himself drawn to David's writings. How he loved to read of David's life in the Samuel scrolls and to compare those stories with the psalms David composed. He had much in common with the son of Jesse.

The changes in John's heart prompted him to begin to plan his move out of the wilderness. Infrequent forays into local villages put him in contact with Hebrew shepherds and an assortment of caravan traders passing through. These rare encounters convinced him that the world was in moral and spiritual decay. His growing respect for the holiness of God merely aggravated the disgust he felt for the decline of Jewish society and the Gentile culture. With anger welling up inside, John often found himself muttering imprecations as he went about his daily tasks.

It was as if the sand in an hourglass had run out. The time of his release from wilderness life was at hand. Organizing his few possessions, he prepared to transfer his base of operations to the Jordan River. He would live closer to people, preaching the message he had been learning for thirty years. A fire burned within to tell of the holiness of God and the dreadfulness of sin and to urge others to live lives demonstrating repentance.

With his bedroll, a change of clothing, and his scrolls under his arms, John left "home" to fulfill his calling. Knowing that the Word of God had come to him, sure that he would preach, and certain that now was the time, John headed for the Jordan . . .

How God Prepares His Servants for Ministry

The biography of John the Baptist may be one of the most neglected of any character study in Scripture. Understanding John's story provides immense help in comprehending the night shift experience in Scripture and recognizing its impact on our own lives. How differently would we approach suffering if we understood the finer nuances of affliction contained in these marvelous sketches? The stories of Jeremiah, Moses, and David are all essential if we are to fully appreciate the biblical teachings on suffering. But it is John who models for us Stage Four of the night shift cycle—the utter necessity of placing the Word of God as the central pillar of one's ministry.

When I graduated from seminary in 1972, I never imagined that, some twenty years later, I would be reflecting on hardship, disappointment, and pain as well as joys and blessings. To be sure, there have been many dividends received during those twenty-nine years; but in retrospect, the unpleasant memories often seem to take center stage.

As I have passed the two-thirds stage of my life and prepare to harness all of my energy and resources for the stretch run, I see my training and preparation much differently than in earlier days. I exited the doors of seminary with my diploma under one arm, signaling a thumbs up, and shouting (metaphorically, of course), "Here I am, Body of Christ!" Like a trained athlete, I envisioned my ministry to be one long marathon with a victory lap thrown in at the end and gold medals cascading over the front of my sweaty jersey.

How wrong of me to think that those seminary years were my "training." In reality, *God chose to use most of my life to train me*. Much of the time, my divinely prescribed training regimen kept me jogging in place. Sometimes I wondered if that restraint was God's preparation for one final sprint down the backstretch. And then I ask myself, "Would He actually expend five decades of my life in preparation for one final frantic dash for the finish line?"

The truth is stark but unavoidable. It could be no other way for, in reality, when I graduated from seminary, *I had no message to preach*. Oh, I was certainly as well trained as a seminary graduate can be, but something was missing. I didn't know this at the time but God did, and so He sent me to further graduate school — His vineyard night classes. It was on the night shift, after more than twenty years of difficult lessons, that I would receive a message from God's Word and emerge with something to say to needy people.

John's story can stretch one's credulity to the breaking point. This man spent roughly thirty years alone in the wilderness for about six months of public ministry. That makes little sense to those of us who operate with a different idea of how to use one's lifetime wisely. Humanly speaking, John's short allotment of time seems tragically squandered.

This scenario is based on a few simple texts of Scripture that provide the outline of the hermit's biography:

His training: "And the child [John] continued to grow and to become strong in spirit, and he lived in the deserts until the day of his public appearance to Israel" (Luke 1:80).

His message: "The word of God came to John, the son of Zacharias, in the wilderness" (Luke 3:2).

His commissioning: "There came a man sent from God, whose name was John" (John 1:6).

His death: "He [Herod] sent and had John beheaded in the prison" (Matt. 14:10).

These portions of Scripture set the parameters of the story of a man whose life reads like that of a failure. Who would want to hire a man apparently lacking in the most basic credentials necessary for success in civil society?

Here's how John's resumé might look:

Heritage: Levite; good stock but limited parental supervision; given great freedom at an early age.

Education: Self-taught; no formal classroom education; reading narrowly confined to Hebrew religious scrolls.

Vocational training: Lived in the wilderness for the first thirty years of his life; excellent survival skills.

Work experience: Has held only one "job"; served six months in an aborted prophetic ministry; self-employed; has not demonstrated the ability to work in a group setting or to submit to authority.

Focus groups: Well received by the poor and common people; refuses to cooperate with the affluent and politically correct.

Criminal record: Served time for defaming a public official; showed no remorse.

Weaknesses: Short-tempered, dour, terse, doesn't work well in groups, melancholic, needs new wardrobe, ascetic, doesn't socialize well.

Strengths: Truthful, honest, righteous, pure, fearless, reliable, good independent worker, can live on small budget, teetotaler.

References: Only Jesus of Nazareth can attest to his character.

Finally, John's obituary might read like this:

After only a brief period of ministry, was imprisoned by Herod in Machaerus Prison, his crime that of confronting a powerful politician for his adultery. Acting on the whim of a dancing girl and her diabolical mother, that politician beheaded him. John's prophetic ministry was a six-month, ill-fated struggle to expose sin and to prepare the way for the

Messiah, who was Himself to be executed by the state after barely three years of public ministry.

John's peers could very well have viewed his life as an extravagant waste. Rather than admiring him, our society would judge John as intolerant and reject him as a misfit and a failure. He surely could have accomplished more through tact and diplomacy, couldn't he?

As I contemplate John's three decades on earth, however, I think I may be detecting a pattern. Hmmm, let me see . . . Joseph spends a few decades as a slave in Egypt before he rises to power and is used by God. Moses spends forty years of his life as an Egyptian trainee and another forty shepherding in the wilderness, all in preparation for a final forty-year whirlwind tour of service to God and His people. David is "on the lam" for more than a decade as a fugitive before he is able to rightfully ascend to the throne of Israel.

Note the similarities: Like an interminable wait in the doctor's waiting room, each of these people also entered God's Waiting Room. They, too, thought they had an "appointment" with God where they would receive His undivided attention. These saints sincerely believed God should be punctual and operate on their time system. Surely each must have reasoned, *God will let me know how long this will take. Since I haven't heard from Him, I guess I'll be off the night shift in no time.* But God, just like a busy professional, is quietly and mysteriously working in another room, out of sight. He doesn't yell, "Yoo-hoo! I'll be right there!" It seems that other, more important things have claimed the divine attention for incredibly long stretches of time while we languish, seemingly forgotten, in the darkness.

Martyrs or Misfits?

The Bible is a record of many "failures" who show up on the pages of the sacred text for what appears to be a mere nanosecond, only to vanish from view. To the undiscerning, these anonymous saints seem to have achieved little or nothing of significance. Many lived lives of excruciating pain, loneliness, and rejection. Some of these individuals are so obscure that we don't even know their names! For example, note the mysterious Hebrew maiden who advises Naaman, the Syrian soldier, on a cure for his leprosy (2 Kings 5). We know the name of the pagan foreigner, but the young damsel who saved his life while living in servitude on foreign turf remains unidentified.

Didn't these individuals have aspirations, hopes, and dreams like others? Did they enjoy their anonymity? Did they construe their life to be a mere blip on the screen of human history? How would their peers have assessed their lives? Were their "careers" wasted? Did they even have careers? Are they human irrelevancies, non-persons to man and God? Or does this give us insight into the mind of God and how He views time and people? Yes, I think there is a pattern here.

Oh, to know what went on in the life of John the Baptist in the decades that he spent alone in the wilderness! We can answer that question only by observing John's life and message when he emerged from "Wilderness Theological Seminary" at the age of thirty. He was simple, visionary, terse to the point of tactless, passionate, fearless, an iconoclast, and, most crucial of all, *he had a message*.

Here is the key text for John: "The word of God came to John" (Luke 3:2). This ferocious icon of integrity suddenly bursts upon the Judean landscape like a spiritual bulldozer. Lowering his blade, John rips into the complacent soil of the religious and common populace with his scathing and relentless declaration of righteousness, honor, and repentance.

Upon leaving the wilderness, John had a sermon that was uniquely his own. We may readily recognize that he had a ministry while failing to notice that *his ministry was his message*. With no message, John's ministry would have collapsed faster than one can swallow a locust coated with wild honey!

Meticulous Bible students have noted many parallels between John the Baptist and the distinguished prophet Elijah. Elijah is said to have begun his ministry, like John, in the wasteland east of the Jordan. In this barren wilderness, the precipitating factor in launching Elijah's ministry was the Word of the Lord (1 Kings 17:2, 5, 8, 14–16, 20, 22, 24; 18:1). Since speaking for

God is the highest calling of any believer, and since proclaiming God's message is the mandate for all disciples, the Word of God beckons us so that we might have a ministry that accomplishes His purposes.

Those delivered from the pit characteristically find that God has answered them by giving them something to say. In Psalm 34, a psalm written (according to the heading of the psalm) after David's escape from the Philistines (1 Sam. 21:10–15), David indicates that he will speak of his deliverance and that others will hear this: "My soul shall make its boast in the LORD; the humble will hear it and rejoice" (Ps. 34:2). David's travail under cover of darkness resulted in a benefit: he now has a message for his listeners.

Psalm 40:3 bears strong testimony to this principle when the psalmist declares, "He put a new song in my mouth, a song of praise to our God." The answer to the Lord's servant laboring on the night shift is the Word of God. If godly saints like Elijah, John, and David have anything to tell us, it is that without the Word of God there is no ministry.

In His Time

God knows the best time to talk to us. There's a popular praise chorus that says,

> I must wait, wait, wait on the Lord;
> I must wait, wait, wait on the Lord;
> And learn my lessons well,
> In His timing He will tell me,
> What to do, where to go, what to say. [1]

Scribbled on the back flyleaf of one of my Bibles are the words of this chorus. Underneath, I recorded this notation: PHC, 6/14/92. I remember June 14, 1992, as if it were yesterday

---

[1] "We Must Wait (On the Lord)," by Randy Thomas. © 1979 Maranatha! Music (Administered by THE COPYRIGHT COMPANY, Nashville, Tenn.). All Rights Reserved. International Copyright Secured. Used by permission.

because three difficult experiences during my stint on the night shift occurred shortly before this date.

First, in early May, my left foot was mangled in a vicious encounter with our lawn mower. This accident didn't require the loss of any of my limbs, although my big toe was severely damaged, five bones were broken in my foot, and I needed a skin graft from my hip to aid in the healing. During this period our family barely survived financially through my work as a bus driver. Now unable to drive, I was out of work without health insurance and with no income for two months.

One week later, I saw my oldest son leave home to join the Navy. The emotion of saying good-bye under such conditions was almost more than I could bear.

Finally, a couple of weeks later, our dog was killed by a tow truck in front of our house. At home alone at the time and nursing my wounded foot, it was my lot to carry our beautiful Labrador retriever inside and hold her in my arms as she died. These three experiences may seem unrelated and relatively insignificant to you. However, as I was barely into my thirty-month night shift assignment, I could already feel the tentacles of the pit closing tight around me.

Now, two days before my forty-sixth birthday, with more than half of my expected life span exhausted, I was doing some serious introspection. Displeased with how the first half of my life had been spent, I felt I had good reason to be less than optimistic about the remaining portion. A Bible teacher with a heart for the instruction of the Word of God, I was "on the shelf" with all doors to ministry slammed shut. My emotions were as low as an upbeat, optimistic, Type A choleric's passions can sink!

June 14, 1992, was a Sunday, so I was in church with my family at Pleasant Hill Chapel (thus, "PHC"). As worship songs were sung, the words of the chorus "In His Time" flashed on the screen.

Sitting near the rear and feeling deeply discouraged, I met God at that moment in the singing of a simple praise chorus. I rarely write such things in my Bible, but the perception that God was speaking to me was so vivid that I felt compelled to record it. In a way similar to John's reception of God's Word, "a message from God came to Dave Shive on June 14, 1992, at Pleasant Hill Chapel." For months, while I cried out to God, I detected nothing but silence. Now He chose this moment to talk to me. I knew that God, through a simple praise chorus, was making a point. If His voice were audible, His words would have sounded something like this:

> *Dave, this is your Lord. You're in a pit and you want out. But I'm in charge. My sense of timing is different from yours, and I'm doing something important in your life while you're on the night shift. You have no clue as to what I'm up to. So just wait for My timing. Forget your age, your schedule, your finances, and all the things that concern you so much. I'll know when you're ready. Then, and only then, I'll show you what to do, where to go, what to say.*

This entire chorus beautifully captures many of the key issues of the night shift. But for our purposes here, permit me to emphasize one idea of the refrain: In His timing He will tell me what to say.

The Holy Word of God is a tapestry woven from many varicolored threads and containing distinctive patterns. Our reading of the Bible may often be cursory and our grasp of biblical truth may prove to be thin and shallow. And yet this amazing God with His incredible Word calls us to be the bearers of His prized message!

And so, while we may gush doctrines and biblical concepts, all the while thinking that we are knowledgeable and effective, God in heaven may be waving His hands and saying, "No! No! You've missed the whole point! And your timing is off!"

Should it not be that the One who inhabits eternity and oversees the universe would want a unique message to be proclaimed by individuals whose hearts are seared by the Scriptures in a manner that forever alters their ministry? Should not this God recognize the hollowness of our words and the missed beats of our lives? Should not He have to tell us what to say—and when to say it—if we are to be useful?

Divine Economics

My friends from the Carolinas tell fascinating stories of growing up in the South. Sharing anecdotes of hog farming, these learned individuals explain how absolutely nothing was ever wasted in the slaughtering of a hog. Everything on the pig was useful in some way, even the intestines, the blood, and the hooves.

In similar fashion, I see God as a People Farmer, of sorts. Granted, the analogy breaks down rather quickly. Nevertheless, it is apparent that God wastes nothing in His developing of godly persons. While we tend to give less value to the painful, difficult portions of our lives, the Bible's advice is practically profound and theologically astute: "Don't discard those night shift experiences! Since God wastes nothing, neither should you."

With this principle in mind, we can echo Paul's thought:

For momentary, light affliction is producing for us an eternal weight of glory far beyond all comparison (2 Cor. 4:17).

There is a "divine intent" for all of God's people. Our God is not wasteful of the experiences, the sufferings, of His children. He discards no experiences, time, or situations when working under cover of darkness to perfect His people. He is the Great Economist, effectively using everything that comes our way.

We labor in the slaughterhouse of our lives, snipping, cutting, and slicing, disposing of that which we consider unusable. "Ah, that event was a waste of time!" we casually remark, tossing it onto the rubbish pile. "That experience was a squandering of resources!" How differently we would view those experiences were we to understand that each one we consign to our experiential landfill was actually a significant part of the divine plan for shaping our message and preparing us to speak to our audience.

As we eagerly discard our debris, our God, Great Economist that He is, comes along behind us, snatching up everything in His arms. He sees the precious treasures we have so nonchalantly jettisoned. Intending to display His glory, He redeems and utilizes every pain, every sorrow, every tear, every trauma, and every disappointment of our lives. What a great and wonderful God, who salvages our garbage from the trash bins of our lives and transforms it into trophies to His grace! Our knowledge of this principle enables us to accept the most difficult circumstances, for "we know that God causes all things to work together for good" (Rom. 8:28).

The Answer Is a Message

What, specifically, is the divine intent of your night shift tour of duty? If John's story teaches us anything, it tells us that God took thirty years *to give John a message:* "The Word of God came to John, the son of Zacharias, in the wilderness" (Luke 3:2).

From 606 to 586 B.C., with Jerusalem and Judah collapsing before the armies of Nebuchadnezzar, many Jewish leaders and families were deported to Babylon. Generation after generation of descendants of those Jewish deportees was born and died in Babylon. Over 125 years later, one of those descendants, a godly man named Ezra, whose story is told in Ezra 7–10 and Nehemiah 8, arrived in Jerusalem after a long journey from Babylon. All who read this account are impressed with his credentials, for Ezra was a true scholar of the Word of God, skilled in the Scriptures and ready to spiritually build the residents. We may take this for granted and, in failing to probe deeper into Ezra's background and training, we could easily miss the most important principle that this learned man has to teach us.

What did Ezra bring from Babylon to Jerusalem? How did he come to possess the knowledge of God's Word and the skill to teach it to others? The conclusion is inescapable. While in Babylon, Ezra was a serious student of the Law.

While in exile, Ezra logically could have concluded that there was no purpose in study or scholarship. Instead, he diligently mastered God's text so that he was prepared to give the people in Jerusalem the one thing they most needed. Therefore, Ezra comes to Jerusalem with a message and the skill and passion to communicate it effectively.

Further, if the text of the Bible pertaining to Ezra's ministry tells the full story, it becomes apparent that *the only thing Ezra does is study and teach the Word of God.* We may see this most clearly by noticing Nehemiah's ministry in contrast with Ezra's work. Ezra arrived in Jerusalem some fourteen years prior to Nehemiah's appearance on the scene.

What will Nehemiah, the Renaissance man, the paragon of construction supervisors, find when he arrives at Jerusalem? Surely Ezra has had sufficient time to rebuild some walls and gates or, at minimum, fix the place up a little bit! No, we have not a shred of evidence that Ezra built or repaired anything during his years in Jerusalem preceding Nehemiah's arrival. Instead, some 140 years after the Babylonian destruction of Jerusalem, and after Ezra's fourteen-year ministry in Judea, Nehemiah receives the report that "the wall of Jerusalem is broken down and its gates are burned with fire" (Neh. 1:3).

Nehemiah gets to work, fulfilling the calling God wired him to accomplish, seemingly unconcerned that Ezra has done no building. The reason is simple: Both Ezra and Nehemiah had drunk deeply from the heart of God and were driven with a passion. Nehemiah could not resist the temptation to organize and build; that was his instinct. And Ezra could not help but teach; in fact, that's all he could do. When the time came for spiritual revival, that great awakening in Jerusalem (recorded in Neh. 8) was not led by Nehemiah, the builder, but by Ezra, the scholar. How good of God to give Ezra a message to proclaim! He teaches us not to waste our "captivity" but to maximize that time when we are on the back burner of God's kitchen.

The importance of a *message* cannot be overestimated. Godly men like Ezra, John, and Jeremiah, great servants of God, illustrate the necessity of having something from the Lord to say to a needy audience. In the case of Jeremiah, it is foolish to ignore the central issue of his life: God *speaks* in and through the pit experience. More than 370 times, in the fifty-two chapters of the Old Testament book that bears his name, Jeremiah mentions that God spoke to him. This is an astounding statistic. The weeping prophet, engulfed in the misery of the final years of Judah, living in Jerusalem under siege, beaten and imprisoned, cruelly rejected, is one-dimensional in his ministry. Every day, he arose to pursue the vocation to which God called him. Going to his workshop, Jeremiah opens his tool box and discovers that only one instrument is available to him: God's voice. He "only" wields the Word of God!

When Jeremiah speaks to the residents of Jerusalem under Babylonian siege, he has God's message for them. When Jeremiah has an audience with King Zedekiah, he tells the monarch what God has to say. If Jeremiah teaches us anything, it is that God has a message for His people and this message must be spoken, no matter what the cost. In his own sufferings in the pit, Jeremiah hears from God. Then, sent to others in their affliction, Jeremiah delivers the message to them.

"A Word from the Lord"

We live in a day when the value of the Scriptures is often demeaned and trivialized. "Head knowledge, intellectualism, facts," some mock, suggesting that serious study of the Word of God will deaden the soul and hinder the Spirit. Like the false prophets and the unqualified shepherds of Jeremiah's day, these diminishers of the Word of God feed God's starving people a diet of empty calories.

It is a spiritual felony for leaders in Jesus' Body to substitute spiritual pabulum for solid food, slowly depriving God's famished flock of precious spiritual nutrients. By implying that less study of the Bible is needed, or that we can somehow bypass Scripture, or that we can add to the Word of God, or that God will speak in other ways apart from His written Word, the Voice of the Living God is suppressed. These false prophets rob hungry people of the vitamin-rich diet needed to endure the night shift. But is there really any other way to know we are hearing from God? If we don't get His message from His Word, from whence will it come? And how do we distinguish God's message from our own if the voice doesn't originate in the Bible? Wise pit dwellers delve desperately and deeply into the Bible, for to fail to hear from God is a catastrophe of the highest degree.

In the aftermath of night duty, there will be a message from God. Would not pit people willingly endure a season

under cover of darkness if the yield were the precious commodity of the Word of God, etched permanently and powerful-
ly on their hearts?

I left seminary in 1972 as a twenty-six-year-old dynamo, full
of ideas, creativity, energy, and courage. But I was an unbroken
man who had precious little to say in the light and much to learn
in the darkness. How was I to know that there would be many
years of hard labor at night to put a message in my heart and on
my lips?

On the other hand, what pastor would say no to a stint on
the night shift if he understood that he would emerge with a fire
in his vocal cords that would be God's message, burning with
such intensity he must preach it lest he die? Is it possible that
pastors, in particular, endure difficulty and affliction for this very
reason? God knows best what thin words His shepherds naturally have to speak. With this deficiency in mind, He subjects His
spokesmen to the rigors of pit time. From within the crucible of
suffering, flawed humans can stand before their needy people,
owning a message of substance and proclaiming it with passion
and conviction.

Fire in Your Heart

It is interesting to note that the imagery of burning is Jeremiah's metaphor of choice to describe the impact of the Word of
God on his own heart (Jer. 5:14; 20:9; and 23:29). Out of the
charred embers of the cauterized heart comes a fiery message,
received in the pit but spoken by "vessels of clay" to others desperately waiting to hear from God.

The coming of the Word of God to him ended John's thirty-
year training period. This "word" is the Greek term *rhema*, not
the typical *logos*. *Rhema* usually implies a specific message
and, in John's case, indicates that he had a particular point to
make to his audience. The emphasis of his message would be
repentance and he would preach it with authority and power
because he had been to God's Night School. The timing was
perfect, John learned his lessons well, and his audience was set
to hear him preach.

You are a "preacher in process" and your audience will be ready when you are. Whether it is coworkers on the job, a Sunday school class, children in the home, a spouse, neighbors, relatives, a youth group, or the person in the next hospital bed, your audience awaits you. This "congregation" of yours desperately needs the Word of God. As surely as any character in Scripture was dispatched by God with a message, you, the pit survivor, have two assignments from on high: (1) learn the Word of God under cover of darkness, and (2) give God's Word to your audience regardless of the shift to which you are assigned.

Consequently, it should not surprise us that our varied pit experiences are intended to prepare us with an uncommon message that only we can give to an audience to which God individually calls us. To fail to hear the message while in the pit is to squander a divine appointment. And there is no competition among the vineyard workers, since you have a message that only you can preach to an audience no one else can reach! Upon deliverance from the night shift, the divine intent can be realized because the delivered one has a message to offer, just as did Jeremiah and Moses and John and Joseph. . . .

A plea for God to speak so we might speak:

Dear Lord, I thank You that You are a God who loves to speak to Your children. As I come to Your Word for refuge, I invite You to burn a message into my heart. Use my time on the night shift to teach me more about Your ways so that I can have a message to give to others. Amen.

He brought me forth also into a broad place;
He rescued me, because He delighted in me.
Psalm 18:19

This poor man cried
and the LORD *heard him,*
and saved him out of all his troubles.
Psalm 34:6

This will be written for the generation to come,
that a people yet to be created may praise the LORD.
For He looked down from His holy height;
from heaven the LORD *gazed upon the earth,*
to hear the groaning of the prisoner,
to set free those who were doomed to death,
that men may tell of the name of the LORD *in Zion*
and His praise in Jerusalem.
Psalm 102:18–21

The appointed time has come.
Psalm 102:13

STAGE FIVE
THE DELIVERANCE

Joseph and the Divine Intent
(Gen. 50)

Joseph surveyed the pathetic scene. His brothers were scheming again, but this time he would have laughed were it not so tragic. "Honest, brother," Simeon was earnestly explaining, palms outstretched, "before he died, Dad told us he hoped that you would forgive us for what we did to you." Turning to Reuben, Simeon nudged him with his elbow and asked, "Isn't that right? Isn't that what Dad would have wanted?"

Obviously reluctant to be a part of this conversation, Reuben replied, "What? Oh, of course . . . er . . . umm . . . yeah, that's right, Joseph. Dad wouldn't want any hard feelings." He and the others shuffled uneasily, eyes fixed on the floor.

Joseph's heart began to ache. His brothers didn't understand what he had learned through the years. God's ways had become so clear to him through his experiences of the past few decades that he longed for others, especially his own family, to appreciate the greatness of his God.

113

He could place the day it all began to come together for him. Though he had felt angry and betrayed by his brothers, it wasn't in the hole in the ground where they had thrown him that he first began to make sense of the divine puzzle. Nor was it on the terrifying caravan trip from Beersheba to Egypt after they sold him into slavery.

The discovery actually began in Potiphar's house. Joseph's owner, a high official in Pharaoh's government, promoted Joseph to chief steward over all of Potiphar's affairs. The Hebrew slave was understandably mystified by his prosperity. Why was he doing so well when other slaves were not shown special favors? There had to be an explanation. He had been honored for some unseen reason. As he wrestled with that question each day, the answer gradually began to dawn on him: God was prospering him! His success was because of *God*.

Joseph's betrayal by Potiphar's wife, leading to his incarceration, had been a deep valley for him. He could still remember that dark season in the dungeon. He asked why a thousand times. Feeling abandoned, Joseph despaired of ever having a life of meaning or joy. But in the midst of the pain, he could not forget how God had blessed him. There had been, even then, a growing conviction that God's hand was on his life and that there would be more blessing.

The rest of the events since his release were a blur to Joseph as he stood before his brothers. The butler and the baker episodes and the grief he felt when he was forgotten in the dungeon seemed a distant memory, as if they had happened in another lifetime. The elation of being freed from confinement and the euphoria of being able to interpret Pharaoh's dream were also cloudy reminiscences.

Now, looking at his brothers, he could not forget the developing awareness deep in his heart that God was doing something big. Joseph had come to a profound conviction that the sorrow and pain he experienced were for some grand purpose, that a divine plan was unfolding.

Every piece of the puzzle was in place, but his brothers still didn't get it. The famine had come and gone as had the years of plenty; and yet here they were—fearful, petty, selfish, not comprehending the incredible love and wisdom of God.

How could he make them see that the cycle of experiences he had endured came from the hand of a sovereign God who was kneading the dough of his life according to His own plan? Was it possible that they could understand what he learned without undergoing the painful experiences he endured?

Joseph raised his hand and his brothers fell silent. Beads of sweat formed on Asher's forehead. Levi comforted Dan, who appeared to be close to tears. Naphtali's normally ruddy complexion had taken on a ghastly hue. They were all expecting the worst. Severe punishment at the least, perhaps even execution.

"Many years ago," Joseph began, "you did an evil thing to me. You sold me as a common slave." Zebulun edged toward the door until he saw a burly Egyptian guard blocking the way. "Through the years," Joseph continued, "I've learned a powerful lesson. I now know that you meant evil toward me, but God intended it for good."

Disbelief marked the faces of his brothers. *Good? God meant their dastardly deed for good?* Stunned, they eyed Joseph, then one another.

Joseph continued. "You thought you sold me to slave traders, but it was really God who sent me to Egypt. He was behind the whole thing. Every part of it was God. He was using you to achieve His own purposes. Don't you understand?"

With those comments, Joseph came to his brothers, embracing each of them in turn. "I forgive you," he said, naming each one. "Don't worry about a thing. We have a great God! He meant it all for good."

The Joseph Principle

Joseph's story is powerful because it illustrates a priceless night shift theorem: When all is said and done, the night shift is about God. It is God who allows any possible pit, permits affliction to come our way, and finally, determines when, where, why, and how to deliver us. Whether or not God ordains or permits all suffering, we know that He sovereignly uses it. Carefully managing the night shift cycle from beginning to end, He allows affliction to beset us and then wields His sovereign power to turn it into good. God ends suffering when He knows the timing is right, delivering the afflicted one in the best way and at the proper time. Using the events surrounding the night shift to achieve His purposes, God teaches us the lessons we need to learn.

Here is the "Joseph Principle": *The night shift is God's method of sovereignly using man's sin, Satan's schemes, and unpleasant natural circumstances to achieve great goals in the lives of His children.*

The term "sovereignty of God" takes on fresh significance when darkness is the topic of conversation. We easily say, "Of course, God is sovereign," but the theory of the night shift cycle stretches to the max our commitment to this biblical principle. The strands that hold our theological systems together are taut with tension when the gloom of darkness tests us. Here God's jurisdiction over our lives moves from the arena of abstract theory to proven trust and faith. When we enter deep levels of suffering, we ask, "Is God really in control when man is at his worst and we are suffering for it?" When heaven is silent, we brood over the possibility that God could lose control, even for a brief moment. If the psalmist pondered God's "fragile" memory, as in Psalm 42:9, 44:24, and 88:1-12, we may also speculate that He could forget about us.

As already suggested, a belief in the sovereignty of God during night shift experiences does not necessarily cast God in the role of precipitator of all suffering. The mother who stands beside her child's casket does not have to conclude that, "Because God is sovereign, He killed my baby." But the sovereignty of God assures us that the event He allowed, He could have prevented. And the tragedy He does not prevent, He will use for His glory and for human good since He makes all things turn out for good.

The Joseph Principle is absolutely crucial. Without adequate appreciation of our Lord's supreme role in our affliction, we cannot fully measure the largeness of the deliverance He provides for us. If God is not to be credited with the night shift, how can we be certain that it is proper to give Him recognition for our deliverance from it? If there is even one tiny detail of this cycle that is beyond God's guidance, can we give thanks in *everything*? And if we are not conscious of His deliverance, the "new song" of Psalm 40 is never learned or properly sung.

Deliverance can seem like such a simple issue; i.e., "I was in trouble and God got me out." But the Bible conveys a richness of thought on the matter of deliverance that does not allow us to reduce the topic to a sound bite. In thinking biblically about the wonder and importance of deliverance, six questions will enable us to probe more deeply into God's perspective on liberation from the darkness.

What Is the Essence of Deliverance?

Deliverance is Abraham, discovering that he does not have to take his son's life. It is Joseph, a slave, being promoted to the highest post in the land of Egypt. It is Moses, standing in awe as the hand of God divides the Sea of Reeds and allows the Israelites to cross over on dry land. It is Samson, bringing down the pillars of a Philistine temple. It is David, the shepherd boy, being crowned king by the elders of Judah and Israel. It is a leper, feeling the compassionate touch of the Master's hand. It is Peter, a fisherman, preaching with power and liberty on the Day of Pentecost. It is Paul, finding immense evangelistic freedom though under house arrest in Rome.

In all cases, deliverance involves the night shift. There is no deliverance without a prior pit. Deliverance is God's exclamation point affixed to the end of the "sentence."

Notice how two psalms, 40 and 118, describe this place of deliverance. In Psalm 40, the terminology of deliverance is vivid: "He brought me up out of the pit of destruction, out of the miry clay, and He set my feet upon a rock making my footsteps firm" (v. 2). For David, the place of rescue is the antithesis of the pit. He was in mire and mud; now delivered, he stands on a solid rock. The rock would have little significance to him had he not first experienced the misery of the mud. The nature of deliverance is to find yourself where you have longed to be: out of the pit and on solid ground.

Although Psalm 118 has David's "fingerprints" all over it, we don't actually know who wrote this psalm since no author's name is attached to it. Our familiarity with the expression in verse 24, "This is the day which the LORD has made; let us rejoice and be glad in it," endears this psalm to us and has given many believers great encouragement. However, one verse does not a psalm make and, in the case of Psalm 118, there is much more behind this little document.

Psalm 118 is a psalm of deliverance. *What is this day that the Lord has made?* we might ask. Reading the psalm to get some context on verse 24, we are amazed to discover the wealth of night shift instruction found here. While it is in one sense true that we may say, "Every day is the day that the Lord has made," the *day* in view here is not a twenty-four hour period of time but the *season* of deliverance. The "day which the LORD has made" is the period of relief after night work, for the psalmist has been through the season of chastening (vv. 5–13, 18) and the season of rejection (v. 22) and now has seen the Lord's work (v. 23) and declares it to be "marvelous." After working at night for a season, what could be more natural than to announce the spectacle of the day that the Lord has made?

Joseph probably never forgot his night shift duty. Long after he rose to the heights of political power in Egypt, he would reflect on the day that his brothers had cast him into the pit. His rise to political power would always be a point of amazement and gratitude to the Lord, for he first had tasted the mud at the bottom of that hole.

Who Is Delivered?

Only those who have endured the pit can know the exhilaration of deliverance. This statement is so simple it seems unnecessary and yet it must be acknowledged. If we want to understand the delight of being rescued, we must attend Night School.

According to the heading of Psalm 34, this song was composed by David fresh off a Night School assignment—his misadventure in Gath where he feigned insanity to save his life. (Read that story in 1 Sam. 21:10-15.) Verse 10 informs us that David was afraid (this is the only narrative text that attributes fear to David). And no wonder! The Philistines of Gath were on to David; they knew who he was and were suspicious of his presence among them. In order to free himself, David pretended to be mentally unfit: he slobbered in his beard and wrote imaginary words on the gate of the city. The ploy worked and King Achish (also known as Abimelech) sent the "madman" on his way. Now, as he sits and pens Psalm 34, David finds that he cannot forget the desperation of that hour:

> I sought the LORD, and He answered me, and delivered me from all my fears. . . . This poor man cried, and the LORD heard him and saved him out of all his troubles. The angel of the LORD encamps around those who fear Him, and rescues them (Ps. 34:4, 6-7).

These are the words of a man who understands the nature of deliverance. David could not have written this song without the lingering memory of night shift assignments and miserable labor in the dark. He remembers that he was terrified and that God delivered him from his fears. So it is that the delivered are marked people. After the night shift, the delivered are transformed.

These songs in the night were written by a man who received an advanced degree in Night School. Drawing upon his storehouse of experience, David is now able to minister to others.

When Does Deliverance Occur?

Why does God deliver *when* He does? By now we have established the fact that God rarely operates on a timetable that makes sense to people. But this is not to suggest that His timetable is whimsical or quirky. We usually can't see how His timing works until after the pit experience has ended and we are just beginning to figure out the reasons that caused God to act as He did.

This is clearly true in Joseph's life. For example, the reason it took so long for Joseph to ascend to power in Egypt was due, in part, to the timing of the famine. In His sovereign wisdom, God anticipated the coming calamity and was preparing His people for survival. In addition, there were many lessons young Joseph needed to learn if he were to be used for God's purposes.

In my younger years, I thought I knew a lot about the ways of God. It was not only that I thought I had figured out what God was doing in my life; I even understood the calendar by which He operated! If I actually had been allowed to develop my own schedule for my deliverance from night shift experiences, everything would have been different. I would have sped through trials and difficulties in record time. My years on the night shift would have been next to nothing. And . . . I would have remained ignorant, immature, and useless.

A rainy day in our household a few years ago served as a sounding board to explore the ways of God. Having just purchased and moved into a new home, we were excitedly unpacking possessions and organizing our lives. Six days later a cloudburst brought us a small but powerful threefold night shift laboratory assignment. First, while I was at work, our newly installed sump pump briefly malfunctioned, causing water to fill one corner of our basement. Simultaneous with this disaster, a hose to our washing machine burst, spraying hot water everywhere. In the big scheme of things, these two unrelated events were minor; but to my wife, home alone with our teenage daughter in a strange house, the solutions to the problems seemed immense and elusive.

The interesting part of this little vignette is that this was a day when the two planned to go to the mall. Becky had been pleading with her mother to take her shopping, but Kathy, inundated with odds and ends, kept delaying their departure. How fortunate that they were delayed. Had they left earlier, our basement and all of our belongings stored there would have been ruined by water. We are sure God looked upon us with favor by keeping mother and daughter in the house long enough to deal with these problems.

I arrived home from work an hour or two later, after the ladies had left for their shopping expedition. Imagine my amazement, upon going to the basement, to find a third problem: a small river of water from the heavy rains was flowing in through the basement wall opposite the sump pump. Although the water made it halfway across the floor, damage was minimal and I was able to keep it from spreading. In subsequent days, I located the causes of this leak and took corrective action. But, like my wife and daughter's delayed departure, my arrival home was timely. Had I been an hour later, or had we made plans to be gone for the evening, these three problems occurring in the span of a few hours would have devastated the proud new homeowners.

It is natural for night shift pilgrims to ask questions about their adversity. For example, I found myself asking: (1) Why did God allow these troubles to occur since we love and serve Him? (2) Why did God let these things happen on this particular day? (3) Where was God when all of this was happening? (4) Why do some people never have leaky basements while I did? (5) Why did God time our departures and arrivals to keep water damage to a minimum while still allowing our family a brief dalliance with the night shift?

Each question is valid, but the fifth is right on the money. We praise God because His divine timepiece is never slow or fast. He does not always prevent trials but delivers us when He knows it will best advance the production goals of the vineyard.

In retrospect, God's timing has always been impeccable. In His perfect wisdom, God often allows me to remain in difficult situations for long seasons, while at other times He has granted swift relief. For lengthy and brief night shift assignments, I am now most grateful. Why does He deliver when He does? Because He is wise, so much wiser than I am!

How Does God Bring About Deliverance?

The technique of God's deliverance is so very wise because He alone understands what has to be accomplished. In 1960, at the age of thirteen, I lost my thirty-four-year-old mother to cancer after she had struggled for over a year with the dreaded disease. During this painful season, the entire Shive family rotated onto the night shift.

121

Before her diagnosis, Mom and Dad were enjoying a wonderful ministry in Dad's pastorate in a small downstate New York town. With three male arrows in the quiver, they were hoping to add a daughter to the crew. And so Mom was pregnant during the last months of her struggle. The baby she was carrying was a little girl, who died about a month before Mom's own death. Humanly speaking, both deaths were senseless.

My father was striving to serve the Lord faithfully. Widowed at forty-one, he found himself attempting to deal with his own grief and loneliness, serve his church, and raise three energetic boys, ages eight, thirteen, and fifteen.

The next five years of my life were dark wilderness wanderings. Although my father was a positive presence in my life, the absence of a mother complicated my attempts at emergence into the adult world. As an adolescent in the throes of normal adolescent struggles, I was looking for spiritual, emotional, and social moorings. Fortunately, this wilderness phase culminated five years later in a personal revival during my first semester in college.

It is indisputable that God can and does heal the sick. But, although we fully recognize that God is capable of conquering cancer or any other ailment, in the case of my mother He chose not to. Mom went to heaven at a crucial time in her life, her family's life, and the church's life.

The mystery of the night shift is that some die and some are healed. For believers, there is no mold to which all suffering conforms. Jacob, who apparently never worked a miracle, died of natural causes at the age of 147 (Gen. 47:28). But then I'm stunned when I read that Elisha, the great miracle-working prophet, simply got sick and died (2 Kings 13:14). Some drivers have auto accidents and never recover. Others have auto accidents and emerge without a scratch. Still others never have auto accidents. We have no clue as to why it happens this way. Only the "secret formula," currently hidden but revealed in Retirement, will give the divine rationale for night shift assignments.

Hebrews 11:35 poignantly bears testimony to this truth. Here the text of God's Word tells us that many believers have been delivered through faith (vv. 32–35a). Others, *by the same kind of faith,* were severely afflicted, apparently without physical relief (vv. 35b–38). The principle in Hebrews 11 hinges on the phrase "and others" in verse 35. While all of God's children ultimately will be delivered from the pain and suffering of this world, there are two aspects to this deliverance: During space and time, some *are* delivered and some *aren't*! Only a sovereign God knows what's best in each situation.

As an aside to my mother's death and to further celebrate the mystery of God's ways, I would mention that my father has been profoundly touched by the tragedy of lost wives in a way that few have experienced. Two years after Mom's death in 1960, he married Maxine, a godly widow with two daughters. Twins were born to my Dad's second marriage. Then, in 1969, "tragedy" struck and Maxine died during childbirth, leaving my father with their five-year-old twins, the two daughters from Maxine's first marriage, and my youngest brother still at home in his senior year of high school.

In 1971 my father married for the third time. This marriage was to Jeanne, another godly woman who had never been married before. They enjoyed twenty-two years of marriage until her shocking death by heart attack in 1993. Finally, in 1995, at the age of seventy-six, my father married Ruth, a wonderful Christian widow, his fourth wife.

Who can comprehend the ways of God? God blesses some couples with forty, fifty, or sixty years of wedded bliss. Other marriages are abbreviated by death, and the spouse who remains is left only with memories. If the sovereignty of God and the trustworthiness of His wise counsel are not the centerpiece of our theology, the pit will devour us with its pain and mystery!

Countless individuals around the world rejoice today in the wisdom of God when He chose not to heed the prayers of thousands for the healing of a young woman paralyzed by a diving accident. As a result, Joni Eareckson Tada has touched many lives. The divine intent was that her disability would achieve a greater purpose than could be accomplished by her healing. Instead of a whole body, God gave Joni grace, a worldwide ministry to the disabled, and the hope in Retirement that her new body will work just fine.

In other words, God delivers in the way He chooses to deliver. Our Lord obviously does not permit everyone who gets sick to die and go to heaven. But He delivered my mother to heaven, assigned my family to the night shift, and eventually delivered me out of my doubt and despair. My mother's passing was ultimately used for good in my life. Additionally, many were touched by her death and exposed to the Gospel through the evangelistic efforts of my father at her viewing and funeral. For each believer, the deliverance will look different, but it is the same God who is accomplishing His purposes as He sees fit.

Why Are We Delivered?

The most magnificent achievement in life is to discover why God is doing the things that He does. For instance, David says, "It is good for me that I was afflicted, that I may learn Your statutes" (Ps. 119:71). One day it must have dawned upon David, *Aha! God allowed me to have these problems to give me a deeper understanding of His principles! Now that makes sense!* It is terribly frustrating to try to process life's difficulties without such insight. The theocentric goal is that we might learn to know God's ways so that He will receive glory.

I can clearly recall the events of January 1956. As a nine-year-old boy, I was captivated by the news of the "tragic" murder of five young missionaries in the jungles of Ecuador. Sorrow and confusion confronted the Body of Christ worldwide as all sought to make sense of the incomprehensible. The lives of five quality young people were "wasted." How awful!

It took years for the full story of the Aucas to be told. Those who have read Elisabeth Elliot's book *The Savage My Kinsman* know that barely twenty months after the death of her husband, Elisabeth returned to live as a missionary among the very people who killed her husband. Additionally, the ranks of volunteers for missionary service swelled dramatically in the months following the Ecuadorian massacre. This is "divine intent."

God brought Elisabeth Elliot onto the night shift to do a work in her that would impact thousands of lives in the following years. The repercussions of those savage murders in 1956 still reverberate around the world! When it is God carrying out His purposes through apparently random, senseless disasters, "waste" and "tragedy" are transformed into blessing.

So it is with the pit. Experiences of suffering are for God's glory. He is working in His children so that His family, the Body of Christ, can bring glory to Him. Joseph clearly understood this and articulated it forcefully to his brothers. When we can say of the miserable experiences we are encountering, "God meant it for good," we are right where God wants us to be!

The night shift sojourner should be warned: Worship, not deliverance, is ultimately the central theme of working in the dark. Since the night shift is "theocentric" (God-centered), not "anthropocentric" (man-centered), deliverance is for God's glory, not man's convenience.

While little children believe that the world revolves around them, mature adults realize that they are but one tiny piece of sand on the human coastline. In the spiritual realm, we may think God's every eternal moment is absorbed with providing peace, prosperity, and ease to His children. The night shift cycle will alter this immature way of thinking. The truth is more painful but profoundly liberating: Genuine brokenness comes to us when the adoration of God becomes more important to us than our own comfort. Wherever we find believers more concerned about personal needs than God's glory, we find need for new night shift rosters to be posted on the vineyard bulletin board.

Encountering the grace of God provides us with a good reason to worship. The greatest potential worshipers are those who have suffered the most. It is these survivors of night work who have the largest exposure to the direct hand of God in graciously delivering them. Jesus' statement, "Her sins, which are many, have been forgiven, for she loved much; but he who is forgiven little, loves little" (Luke 7:47), could easily be paraphrased to read, "Your sufferings, which are many, have resulted in a great deliverance; and he who has been delivered much will give thanks continuously."

Consequently, the night shift, deliverance, and worship are inextricably woven together into the fabric of the cycle of affliction. God delivers for three primary reasons. First, since God suffers with us on the night shift, He is eager to see us delivered. He takes pleasure in our deliverance. Second, because God intends to use us, our deliverance opens doors for us to make fresh impact for the vineyard that He owns.

Third and most important, it is God's intent to deliver us so that we can worship Him. Joseph, perhaps more than any character in Scripture, demonstrates the importance of understanding the issues involved in deliverance from the pit. But his ability to see the "big picture" of what God was doing in the darkness was determined by his understanding of God's sovereignty. Under cover of darkness, Joseph's night vision was astounding. Later, with the wearisome shift behind him, the daylight more perfectly revealed the grand purpose of God in his suffering.

God doesn't deliver just to give relief. As we shall see in Stage Seven, The Impact, deliverance is for the purpose of usefulness. In fact, the whole night shift cycle exists because we are not very useful to God. He longs to promote us, and so we are sent to Night School for further education. This education equips graduates for service. How many individuals has Psalm 7 spoken to over the centuries? Psalm 18? Psalm 32? Psalm 34? Psalm 40? Psalm 51? Each of these songs in the night point us to a purpose for our suffering.

Where Do the Delivered Ones End Up?

If pit people are in the constricted, narrow place, those who have experienced God's marvelous deliverance (in His way, in His timing, for His purposes) will find themselves in the broad place. Ultimately, as I have mentioned before, the broad place is a place of usefulness, the place where impact is made.

He brought me forth also into a broad place . . . . You enlarge my steps under me, and my feet have not slipped. . . . You have set my feet in a large place. . . . From my distress I called upon the LORD; the LORD answered me and set me in a large place (Ps. 18:19, 36; 31:8; 118:5).

The large place is a tribute to the mercy, wisdom, largesse, and power of a sovereign God to bring the poor, weak, and hopeless into a place of usefulness and blessing.

During my thirty-month pit experience, while driving tour buses, delivering oil, and running a lawn care service, it seemed to me an impossibility that I would ever again find myself in full-time ministry. I feared that my resumé was hopelessly besmirched by the myriad of "setbacks" that had come my way. This is merely more evidence of my fear of man and my small view of God. Now, almost ten years after the onset of that pit experience, having pastored a church for six years and served on the faculty of a Christian college for nearly four years, I marvel at my small-mindedness and the amazing God whom I call "Father."

This has been a chapter of hope. It is intended to remind the afflicted that God does deliver, that He, in fact, takes delight in rescuing His children from the miry clay and placing them on the solid rock. For the emancipated, the words of deliverance will echo in their hearts and on their lips: "The sound of joyful shouting and salvation is in the tents of the righteous" (Ps. 118:15). That almost sounds like a "new song" on the lips of the delivered. . . .

A prayer for deliverance:

Heavenly Father, what would I do if I could not trust You in my affliction? I thank You that I can anticipate deliverance from the night shift cycles of my life. I don't know how or when You will step in and change this situation. But I do know that You will do it in the right way and at the right time. I worship You, for You alone are trustworthy. Amen.

You are my hiding place;

You preserve me from trouble;

You surround me

with songs of deliverance.

Psalm 32:7

All my bones will say,

"Lord, who is like You,

who delivers the afflicted

from him who is too strong for him,

and the afflicted and the needy

from him who robs him?"

Psalm 35:10

STAGE SIX
THE NEW SONG

Paul and a Life of Worship
(Acts 16:1–40)

Paul had lost all track of time, but he estimated it to be a little before midnight. There was a faint gleam of moonlight shining through the crack in the wall that served as a window. Looking through the shadows at Silas, stretched on his side against the opposite wall, it was apparent that Paul's partner was also sleepless. No wonder. Hungry and cold, they were both in severe pain from the harsh beating they received that afternoon.

The dungeon in Philippi was pretty typical. Paul had done enough jail time to know that. These small-town jails had a stark simplicity to them—dirty, dank, and dark. He tried not to think of his clean, comfortable, rented room back in Antioch.

Paul was the first to speak. "You awake?" he whispered. Silas grunted in response. "You know, I've been thinking," Paul mumbled through swollen lips. "Here we are in jail again. Years ago I would have dreaded the idea of imprisonment, but I almost feel at home in these cells."

129

"Mmmm," mumbled Silas. "Me, too. It's hard to believe how my attitude has changed. I hate this place. So why am I not complaining?"

Twisting to get comfortable on the hard floor, Paul nodded. "I was such a mess, Silas—totally into myself, arrogant, doing all of the wrong things, I actually thought I was pleasing God. And then Jesus stepped in, blinded me, and then opened my eyes. He changed everything." Then, in a hoarse voice, Paul began a little chorus that he and his companion often sang under better circumstances.

From across the narrow cubicle, Silas stared at his cellmate. *Paul was singing? In this Macedonian jail? What was it about this strange little guy, anyway? Maybe it was those eight years or so he'd spent back home in Tarsus after his conversion.* Although his friend never talked much about that time, Silas knew that Paul had felt pretty useless. In spite of his burning desire to teach and preach, all doors of opportunity had been closed to him.

Or was it that stretch in Arabia? Paul never spoke at all about his season of solitude in the desert. How hard it must have been for such a visionary to be out of action. But God had undoubtedly been at work during those extraordinary times of isolation and tent-making.

Then again, Paul's approach to life could have been honed during those difficult months on his first missionary trek through Asia Minor. Often rejected by Jewish leaders, pagans, and Roman officials, his friend had suffered much for Jesus. More than anyone he knew.

Silas joined in, unaware that he was slightly off-key. Louder and louder the sound swelled as they began a different lyric based on Psalm 40: "He put a new song in my mouth . . . ." Other prisoners began to stir as the entire jail echoed with the sound of joyful music.

A short while later, with Silas snoring deeply, Paul reached for his leather bag and pulled out his quill and ink. Mentally picturing dear believers far away and pressing the parchment flat on the floor, he began to write. "I thank my God whenever I remember . . . ."

Suddenly he felt a vibration. "Pssst, Silas," he whispered. The floor was beginning to tremble. . . .

The Message Is a Song

The sixth stage of the pit cycle is profoundly musical. When John the Baptist emerged from his thirty-year wilderness assignment, Night School had given him more than a degree. He had a tune that was the fruit of the darkness. Without the protracted time of lonely wilderness training, John would have had nothing important to sing about.

David also, upon his discharge from the pit of Psalm 40, found he was singing a new refrain. This song was the product of night shift labors. Over and over he wrote paeans of praise, each one borne of deep valleys, loneliness, doubt, anger, fear, and weariness. Each song tells us something that David learned about God while in the pit. David's theology is not anemic, but healthy, robust, authentic. How deficient his worldview would have been had he not spent that long season on the night shift!

At age forty, Moses was passionate about delivering the Hebrews from bondage. It took forty more years for that passion to die a natural death. Then, at eighty years of age, when Moses left the wilderness to lead his people to Canaan, his obsession had changed. He was a man confronted with the holiness and majesty of God. Stripped of all self-confidence and arrogance through eighty years of failure and defeat, Moses is singing God's praises by the time of the Exodus: "Then Moses and the sons of Israel sang this song to the LORD" (Ex. 15:1).

Singing the Blues

One particular psalm gives a different slant on singing as it views Israel from the perspective of her captivity in Babylon. Prior to their deliverance, the Israelites were compelled by their captors to sing a song of Zion (Ps. 137:3). But they simply weren't in the mood. Brokenhearted, they mumbled the blues: "How can we sing the LORD's song in a foreign land?" (v. 4).

Just as many of the rich songs from the African-American community reflect the funereal pit of slavery, Psalm 137 is part of the heritage of the Babylonian captivity. Indeed, on the night shift, joyful singing is hard work, even incongruous. But the darkness is fertile time for songwriting. Apparently, in the biblical philosophy of the night shift, there is a time when the blues are acceptable church music.

Just hitch a ride with the children of Israel from Egypt to Canaan and listen to some hypothetical exchanges between travel-weary Hebrews:

"Ohhhh! It's ho-t-t-t out here. I'm getting burned real bad in this blazing sun."

"Yeah, and my feet hurt. At least in Egypt we could rest once in a while in the shade! Hey, Moses, how about a break?"

"And how about some water, while you're at it? I haven't had a drink of cool, fresh water in ages. At least back in Egypt we had decent water. I'm sick of this brackish desert stuff."

"Travel a while. Pitch the tent. Sleep. Pack up the tent. Then we travel some more. Been there. Done that. Bo-o-o-ring."

"Yeah. And what about Moses as a desert guide? Hah! He couldn't lead a Nile asp out of Pharaoh's back pocket!"

Can't you faintly hear the mournful wail of a saxophone in the background? Tired, thirsty, fearful, and longing for a few days spent in one place, the Israelites had plenty of good excuses for their miserable attitude. In fact, memories of Egypt had been altered to the point that many were actually longing for a return to slavery in the land of the Nile.

"Would that we had died by the LORD's hand in the land of Egypt, when we sat by the pots of meat, when we ate bread to the full; for you have brought us out into this wilderness to kill this whole assembly with hunger" (Ex. 16:3).

Or, listen to this interaction when the water supply dwindled shortly after leaving Egypt:

"Give us water that we may drink." And Moses said to them, "Why do you quarrel with me? Why do you test the LORD?" But the people thirsted there for water; and they grumbled against Moses, and said, "Why, now, have you brought us up from Egypt, to kill us and our children and our livestock with thirst?" (Ex. 17:2-3).

It takes no imagination or creativity to grumble a sour note or two. Just two chapters earlier, Moses, Miriam, and the entire nation of Israel sang God's praises and danced like there was no tomorrow. Now they are back on the night shift and their memories are short. Memories of deliverance fade fast. It's back to the old song in no time at all.

During the thirty months of my night shift assignment, I went 856 days without preaching, a significant sabbatical from my passion for giving out the Word of God. On top of that, the four different jobs I held—lawn care service manager, tour bus driver, oil truck driver, and college truck driver—paid wages that were far less than I had been making in the ministry. This created exceptional financial strain on my family. Some comments in my journal, dated February 25, 1993, tell of my despair:

What a struggle to keep on doing this when my heart is elsewhere. There are churches and ministries in need and I have something to offer. My peers and friends enjoy full-time ministry, the pastorate, etc., while the Lord keeps all doors closed for me.

There are times at work when I feel shame as I realize the lowliness of my work. Others smile at me as they pass me by while I sense their thoughts—"Poor guy. I'm sure glad I've made something of myself, that I have a future. What sad series of events must have conspired to bring him to this pathetic stage of life?" When I sense that, I reject the shame, knowing I'm doing what's right, the will of God, but I hate it.

In a chapter devoted to praise, why would I recite the sad litany of my past complaints to God? It was during those thirty months that the strong hand of God gripped my life in a way

133

that I could not have anticipated. Out of that night shift experience came a deeper realization of God's greatness and His ways of doing things. This is the way of the cross, the route our Savior trod. Going deep into the valley enabled God to transform my attitude so that I could learn to praise Him.

The New Song

When the darkness has done its job, the singer is drawn to new lyrics with a different sound. Israel's wilderness wanderings—and mine—merely confirm God's wisdom. His people's musical aptitude is undeveloped, so a few semesters in the Night Conservatory under the tutelage of Maestro Moses is needed to sharpen our vocal and instrumental skills.

While Psalm 40 does not specifically record the soundtrack of the "new song," it does suggest two distinct features: (1) the new song is sung after deliverance, and (2) the new song is "praise to our God." In light of this, how inappropriate it seems for believers who have been redeemed by the blood of the Lamb to be singing an old song.

It is patently clear that the one who is delivered from the darkness is to have a message and that each message will be fine-tuned to the individual personality and pit experience. The diligent student who has been delivered from the night shift will go forth to proclaim that message with great enthusiasm.

The common denominator of the message and the new song is that both are words of worship, sovereignly placed on the heart and tongue of the delivered. Who better to grasp the enormity of God's sovereignty, power, and grace than one who has done time on the night shift? That glad proclamation is a song, even if the messenger is tone deaf!

As I have wrestled with Psalm 40 in the past few years, one question surfaces in my mind over and over: *What was David's new song?* I have read and reread this psalm in a quest to figure out the lyrics given to David as part of his post-deliverance message. There are many "new song" ingredients here waiting to be discovered. But I detect two primary messages in Psalm 40 that David might have put to music. See if you agree.

The first is the message of awe.

> Many, O LORD my God, are the wonders which You have done, and Your thoughts toward us; there is none to compare with You. If I would declare and speak of them, they would be too numerous to count (v. 5).

Rather than being bitter over his pain or regretting the "wasted" time spent in the pit, David stands in awe of God. The test of the effectiveness of a night shift experience is whether, after deliverance, we have the proper regard for the Sovereign Lord of the universe. He alone is our Deliverer and we stand before Him, incredulous at His wisdom and His deeds. Where genuine adoration exists, there is evidence that the night shift has done its work.

Our sense of worship is profoundly heightened when we endure affliction. During suffering, our eyes are veiled to whatever wonderful thing God is doing. But in retrospect, deliverance affords the opportunity to say, "Oh, I get it. So *that's* what God was up to. That's incredible! God is so amazing!"

The second message is the lesson of obedience.

> Sacrifice and meal offering You have not desired; my ears You have opened. Burnt offering and sin offering you have not required. Then I said, "Behold, I come; in the scroll of the book it is written of me. I delight to do Your will, O my God. Your law is within my heart" (vv. 6–8).

The wonderful lesson learned by enduring the pit and being delivered from affliction is this: Obedience is best, and the pit teaches us to relish obedience! This is learned because the trauma and grief of the night shift breaks the child of God. The nature of our learning styles is such that we do not truly grasp the most important lessons in life except under compulsion. One may enter the night shift with a casual attitude toward obedience, but the instruction of the darkness will not allow such a mind-set to persist.

Should we not be continuously astounded by the revelation in Scripture that Jesus, the Perfect God-Man, traveled the route of affliction? Jesus apparently rarely rotated off the night shift. And should we not stand in awe that, "although he were a Son, yet learned he obedience by the things which he suffered"? (Heb. 5:8, KJV). So we see that the Father made "the captain of their salvation perfect through sufferings" (Heb. 2:10, KJV). No, this does not suggest that Jesus was disobedient and then had to learn obedience, or that there was any flaw in Him. What the writer of Hebrews is saying is that Jesus experientially learned the trait of obedience through suffering in space and time while living in human flesh. There are lessons that must be learned in the dark, that is, on the night shift. If this was true of Jesus, why should it be any different for us?

Will We Ever Learn?

Entering the night shift, the naive believer may trivialize sin. Euphemisms are tossed about glibly. "Sins" and "transgressions" become "indiscretions," "issues," and "errors." Adultery is "an affair"; lying is a "fib"; stealing, "appropriation." Such careless vocabulary serves as further evidence of our desperate need for night shift duty, where, upon learning of the holiness of God, sin becomes loathsome and a passion for obedience is acquired. On the night shift, the sufferer is shut up with a Holy God who proceeds to work diligently on His child. Lessons of purity, holiness, and obedience are reinforced under cover of darkness.

Having done a self-appraisal and not found ourselves lacking, we may believe that we are fully committed to the Lord. But God's view of things is so much more accurate. He sees the smallness of our thoughts, the immaturity of our outlook, the selfishness of our approach to relationships. Perhaps, like an earthly father who knows his small son or daughter well, God sighs to Himself, "My poor child, you have so much to learn." And as the Perfect Father, He sets out to design a "program" that will effectively change our total outlook.

After graduation from seminary in 1972, I busied myself with the task of ministry, unaware that there were still major aspects of my heart that needed some special Fatherly attention. I was forcibly reenrolled for more credits in God's Night School.

This new lesson was prompted by the fact that, after a couple of years of ministry, I decided to seek ministerial ordination. It is very clear to me today, some twenty-five years after the fact, that this impulsive decision was prompted by immaturity. Like Saul, who could not wait for Samuel to come—and so he chose to proceed with illegitimate sacrifices (1 Sam. 13:8-14)—I did not wait for God's direction. Unlike John the Baptist, I can now see that it was *not* the Word of the Lord that came to me.

While John waited until God burned a message on his heart, I was in too big a hurry. Life was passing me by. After all, I was pushing thirty years of age! People needed me! In spite of the fact that I did not yet have a message that burned like a fire within, I was convinced that the world was eager to hear my thoughts.

An ordination council was arranged. Godly men convened to hear my theology, to question me. When it was all over, I was astounded, outraged, and disheartened to be denied ordination. The council assured me that my educational background was excellent and that I was academically prepared and intellectually ready for their questions. So what went wrong?

The answer that counts is the heavenly perspective. If God had spoken to me audibly that night, it probably would have sounded something like this:

> *Dave, remember Humble Pie 101 and 201? Well, school is back in session. In fact, you're in graduate school, now, and this is Eat Crow 301. I've convened a special group of eminently qualified tutors to teach you this material. These guys are the cream of the crop, men of wisdom, of prayer, very knowledgeable in My Word. I have sent them to rebuff you and reject you. They are My ministers, a special gift to you. I mean this for your good. Best wishes. I'm sure you'll get a passing grade!*

Interestingly enough, as proof that I needed to take this advanced course, my initial response was identical to my reaction to earlier stabs at the Humble Pie curriculum. I was again angry, bitter, and resentful. In the context of Psalm 40 and the lesson of obedience, however, both courses were priceless. My loving Heavenly Father knew me quite well and designed a unique internship for me. Eventually, I was able to be grateful for the decision rendered by that ordination council.

The Freedom of Surrender

As the night shift drags on, God demands and receives more and more of our hearts. We begin to inventory our lives to find things that we may be holding in reserve. The misery of the darkness stimulates us to do a more meticulous review. Up and down the rows of the stockroom of our lives we go, clipboard in hand. Shelves we normally tend to avoid force fresh attention. "Hmm," we mutter, "I didn't know that was still on the shelf. I thought I had gotten rid of that long ago," and, "Wow! Where did that item come from?" We struggle with the need to jettison the excess material cluttering our minds and spirits. And so the night shift process gradually reveals the little nooks and crannies that are yet to be relinquished to the lordship of Jesus Christ.

During further night shift stints endured many years after my ordination council, I repeatedly found myself searching every aspect of my life to see what else I was selfishly clutching. Prying the grubby fingers of my will apart, I was shocked to see that there was still more to surrender to Jesus. As I daily made my rounds in my oil truck, I wrestled with God, angels, and self.

The climax of that night shift experience came when I finally placed on the altar my desire to return to full-time ministry. This final bridge-burning ceremony was no small achievement. I entered the night shift self-confident, absolutely certain that I had surrendered all to Jesus, and determined to return to full-time vocational ministry as soon as possible. It took the deplorable conditions of the darkness to expose the cache I carefully had hidden in the rear of my spiritual stockroom. I was holding more in reserve than I realized or was willing to admit.

As we enter the vineyard to begin work, our spiritual checkbooks are tucked away out of sight. But individuals on the night shift inevitably find themselves taking out their checkbook. Pen in trembling hand, they breathe a sigh of relinquishment as they sign a blank check and place it in the hands of Jesus. The Master has the authority to fill in the amount, taking as much as He wants. Pit time is often what it takes for disciples to open their accounts to such close scrutiny.

So, too, we will discover that there is always more to learn about our Savior and surely more to give to Him. The pit is both a blessing and a benefit, for it is God's classroom to help us discover just how unyielded we really are. The survivor of the darkness now comes to God in utter dependence on Him and with no confidence in the flesh. With the independent will broken, obedience is seen in a different light. Not only does David say he is *willing* to be obedient—no, much more! "I *delight* to do Your will, O my God" (Ps. 40:8). Is your struggle with the joy of obedience? Then the night shift is for you!

This is a lesson to be learned and relearned. Believers who are biblically literate should not be shocked to find that life is a series of shift rotations as the darkness summons us again and again. Deliverance, a cause for great rejoicing, may be interrupted by more night shift assignments. It should come as no surprise that David, after his deliverance, returned to the darkness many times. Jesus languished in the shadows for much of His life, as did Paul. This is the way of the one whose heart is set on following the Father's will.

And this explains why David had so many new songs flowing from his pen. Quite simply, he spent so much time in the well, he was constantly tapping into fresh springs.

A new-song prayer:

> *Holy God, You are so amazing. You have watched over me since my conception in my mother's womb. You have guided my life every step of the way. All of the twists and turns have been directly supervised by You. Even the most painful moment of suffering was under Your watchful eye. I stand in awe of You and sing Your praises. You are so magnificent and worthy of my worship. Hallelujah!*

Then I will teach

transgressors Your ways,

and sinners will be converted

to You.

Psalm 51:13

My soul will make its boast in the LORD*;*

the humble will hear it and rejoice.

Psalm 34:2

I will tell of Your name to my brethren;

in the midst of the assembly I will praise You.

Psalm 22:22

Stage One—The Pit
Stage Two—The Wait
Stage Three—The Cry
Stage Four—The Answer
Stage Five—The Deliverance
Stage Six—The New Song
Stage Seven—The Impact

STAGE SEVEN
THE IMPACT

Peter Learns to Fish
(Luke 5:1–11; Acts 2:14–41)

I rritation virtually oozes from Peter's pores. Although outwardly calm, he is annoyed to think that his Friend would have the audacity to suggest that they launch the boats to do a little fishing. The consummate fisherman, Peter hardly needs a *carpenter* to tell him when and where to fish. When has he ever tried to tell Jesus how to build furniture?

Besides, having fished all night, Peter has sleep on his mind. He and his crew had been repairing the nets and putting equipment away so they could hit the sack when Jesus borrowed his boat for a pulpit. Now a request from the Master to head back out to sea is the last thing they want to hear.

He doesn't let on, but Jesus knows what's churning inside Peter's mind. He can read the blustery big guy like a book, and the Master Teacher knows exactly what He is doing. "Come on, Pete. Let's head for the deep water," Jesus says with a twinkle in His eye.

Knowing that mid-morning is not prime time for casting nets, Peter scarcely manages to suppress his agitation. "Master, we've fished all night and caught nothing." After a second glance at Jesus' determined look, Peter responds with a shrug of his shoulders, "But if You say so. . . ."

Out to sea they go—the eager Carpenter and the disgruntled fisherman. Look at Peter, sitting on the edge of the stern, arms crossed, back turned to Jesus. His gaze is fixed on some distant spot on the receding shoreline. There is no small talk, for this is not a pleasure cruise and Peter is not a happy skipper.

Note Jesus, without a care in the world, sitting in the bow of the boat. He leans back with His face to the sun, the fresh air blowing through His hair. One would think He is unaware of the big fisherman singing the blues at the other end of the boat. Yes, great lessons are in store this fine day.

Finally, Jesus selects the spot and the nets are let down. Peter smirks inwardly. *Ha! What will He do when we catch no fish? He's a great teacher and a wonderful man, but He will soon discover how little He knows about fishing.*

The flood of fish is almost instantaneous. Not initially understanding that there is more than meets the eye here, Peter begins to haul the load aboard. It is soon obvious that he can't handle such a quantity of fish alone, and he motions to his partners to come and help.

It is at this point that something clicks into place. Peter remembers the empty nets of the night before. Standing knee-deep in fish, he lets the nets drop and collapses at Jesus' feet. "O Lord, please leave me!" the fisherman exclaims. "I am a sinful man!"

But Jesus claps Peter on the shoulder in a gesture of affection. "Don't be afraid, Peter." The Master's voice is calm and reassuring. "From now on, you'll fish for men."

* * *

Some time later. . . "Men of Judea, hear these words." Peter could hardly believe his own ears. The crowd stood in rapt attention as he bellowed out his first unpolished sermon in a curious Galilean accent. With almost no formal education or training, Peter was speaking in public. Even more amazing, the people were listening!

"Men and brethren, let me speak freely to you of the patriarch David," Peter began. Though Peter had recently undergone a remarkable metamorphosis, none of his friends ever dreamed they would see this day.

Now it was the evening of Pentecost, and this had been a very long day. It began with a prayer meeting in the upper room with the other disciples and concluded with the open-air gathering and Peter's impromptu sermon. The mass conversion of thousands followed.

Settled in bed in the home of a friend on the west side of Jerusalem, Peter closes his eyes. But sleep is not swift in coming. Mental images parade through his mind. Painful memories of Jesus, being dragged away by soldiers. Peter, standing by a fire, warming himself. Peter, cursing and shouting at the top of his lungs. He had distanced himself from Jesus that dismal night, vigorously denying any relationship whatsoever with his Master.

No human being ever felt more despondent than Peter that dark Passover evening. He roamed the streets of Jerusalem, ducking into alleys and jumping at the slightest sound, until the sun stained the sky with a red glow. An emotional and spiritual wreck, Peter was convinced that God was finished with him. How could he have been so cowardly as to deny the Son of God? Depression and despair gripped his soul.

Then . . . the remarkable events surrounding the resurrection forever altered Peter's life. Jesus commissioned *him*, Peter—the very one who had denied his Messiah—to tend His flock. Today he preached in the name of Jesus and many believed. Once only a poor fisherman, here he was, just as the Master had promised, fishing for men. That he should be used to make a difference in the lives of others was more than a miracle!

Now Peter understands that those painful experiences of just a few weeks ago were crucial to his present usefulness. Formerly an arrogant loudmouth, he now proclaims the truth of the Risen Lord. Jesus should have rejected him, trashed him on the garbage heap of unfaithful disciples. Instead, His Savior forgave him, entrusted a message to him, and allowed him to be a spokesman of the resurrection to thousands. But it took the pit of cowardice, misery, and melancholy to expose his true weakness. . . .

Turning in the narrow bed, Peter pulls the blankets over his shoulders. Before drifting off to sleep, he ponders the awesome reality that impact for the Gospel was made today. The Master actually found him useful!

Usefulness: The Large Place

It is every disciple's Pentecost when the elixir of usefulness is tasted. The cramped confinement of the darkness gives way to intoxicating sunlight and open spaces. Released from the airless narrowness of the pit, the delivered one exults in fresh air, color, aromas, festivity, music—freedom. This is atmosphere tinted by grace.

But before this Pentecost, lessons must be learned. *Some* workers know how useless they are. They lack experience and confidence and have no assurance that they will ever be effective vineyard workers. To be able to serve with power in the light, they must be instructed in the character of God in the darkness.

Other disciples do not know they are useless to the Master. Unbroken and unaware of their condition, these individuals need intensive tutoring in Night School so that their confidence will be in God and not in self.

It is in the darkness that the varied problems that interfere with vineyard production goals are addressed and corrected. Workers emerge from the darkness with a deeper knowledge of the Owner, a greater focus, a clearer understanding of God's Handbook, and an enhanced awareness of the principles that drive the vineyard's operation.

The Owner's grand intention to show kindness to others through His vineyard's productivity is achieved by the education that takes place in the dark. Employees who receive special Night School training are the ones to distribute these goods.

Upon graduation, they will end up in the large place of impact. Uneducated and untrained employees are no asset to such an incredible enterprise as Kingdom Vineyard!

The termination of the night shift cycle—the "large place"—is documented in Scripture: "From my distress I called upon the LORD; the LORD answered me and set me in a *large place*" (Ps. 118:5). "He brought me forth also into a *broad place*" (18:19). "You have set my feet in a *large place*" (31:8).

The metaphor of the large place is an appropriate counterpart to the pit, since release from that hole in the ground means liberation to a place where one can stretch and be free. This is the invigorating return to the day shift, a temporary liberation from working under cover of darkness.

As there is a cycle to the narrowness of the pit, there is also a "cycle of enlargement." When impact occurs and the delivered one is used to touch other lives, the night shift begins to make sense. "Enlargement" enables one to see reasons for affliction.

The Purpose of the Broad Place

The darkness is a hindrance as well as a place of education. In the darkness of their distress, Joseph, Moses, David, Jeremiah, John, Paul, and Peter were temporarily prevented from preaching the message and fulfilling the vision that God gave them. While the darkness is a helpful tool in growth and maturation, it will inevitably suffocate and destroy if deliverance does not come. My time of misery in the oil truck was indispensable to my education, but greater impact was to be found later in my roles as pastor and professor upon my release from the night shift. Only so much work can be done under cover of darkness. The light of day is also vital if God's broader purposes are to be accomplished.

Though one is given a message on the night shift, the venue and audience for that message will often be discovered only after release. Saul's insane jealousy, though immensely influential in shaping David as a man of God, prohibited David from doing what Samuel had anointed him to do. Moses could not free his people as long as he remained in Midian and the children of

Israel lingered in Egypt. Jeremiah's message had minimal circulation while he was restricted to the dungeon. John personally profited from the long wilderness sojourn, but greater society needed to hear him preach in public places. The large place that followed released David and Moses and Jeremiah and John to follow their calling, sing a new song, serve in their divinely appointed venue, and impact their selected audience.

Deliverance is not for personal comfort or enjoyment. The night shift is intended to prepare the child of God to be used for His purposes. Since the night shift is preparatory, the "large place" is the platform for ministry when the survivor of the pit is released to impact others.

Where Angels Fear to Tread

In the spring and summer of 1991, I was shocked to find my spirit deeply shaken. Although I am generally willing to enter where angels fear to tread, at that time I was tossed about by waves of doubt, unbelief, and apprehension.

My later analysis of this fear led me to conclude that two primary worries besieged me. First, I was alarmed at the possibility that I would not be able to find employment in full-time vocational Christian work. Having just resigned my pastorate and observing all ministerial doors closing before me, my panic accelerated and my foreboding increased. How would I support my family? Would I be able to fulfill the dreams that God had given me for the strengthening of the church?

Second, I am ashamed to admit that I was deeply concerned over what others would think of me. After all, I was in ministry for almost two decades. There is unfortunately a certain unspoken but palpable stigma directed at times towards pastors and full-time vocational Christian workers who, for any reason, find themselves in "secular" employment. I discovered that I could not communicate to my friends in the ministry the mysterious nature of my night shift experience. The glazed looks and averted glances of many of these colleagues suggested they were embarrassed for me or simply couldn't comprehend my predicament. Their words of encouragement were few and generally unhelpful.

I am amazed to discover in retrospect that I was afraid of the opinions of others! Even worse, I foolishly feared that humans could keep me from fulfilling the ministry for which God wired me and for which He had been preparing me. In my panicky mind, people carried more clout in organizing the agenda of the Kingdom Vineyard than did the Owner! Even more startling was my fresh realization that great and godly people in Scripture struggled with—even wrote about—this very same problem.

Just as the pit is a place of restriction, the large place is primarily a position of expansive influence. In the small place, movement is contained and access is limited. The muscles atrophy and skills lie dormant. Brain processes deteriorate and conversation is tense and discouraging. Dreams die and hope turns to despair. On the night shift, one turns this way and that, looking for freedom of movement, but there is only confinement and hindrance.

Deliverance to the large place is obviously important to people, but it is equally vital to God's interests, for the message learned in the cramped confines of the small place will bring glory to God when preached in the large place of impact. Emerging from the night shift, we are wiser and better-equipped leaders. God has a lot at stake in our deliverance.

Can Adulterers and Murderers Be Useful?

Impact is the final stage of the night shift cycle. In the words of Psalm 40:3, David is now touching the lives of others in a positive way: "He has put a new song in my mouth—praise to our God; many will see it and fear, and will trust in the LORD" (NKJV).

It is noteworthy to consider another occasion when David emerged from the pit, aware of his increased usefulness. On that occasion he pleaded with God, "Restore to me the joy of Your salvation, and uphold me with Your generous Spirit. Then I will teach transgressors Your ways, and sinners shall be converted to You" (Ps. 51:12–13, NKJV). David spoke these words as an adulterer and murderer.

David's adultery with Bathsheba and his murder of her husband (2 Sam. 11–12) was the pit experience forming the backdrop to Psalm 51. The valley of despair that engulfed David in the days following those evil deeds must have been truly dreadful. He knew too much about God to sin so heinously and then to dismiss his deeds so casually. Living with the ghost of adultery and murder hanging over his head, the troubled monarch found himself enveloped in a spiritual midnight that threatened to destroy him.

Perhaps, in the aftermath of the Bathsheba debacle, he waited with awful anticipation for God to intervene. Every knock on the door was ominous; maybe the next visitor would expose his hideous crimes. *Who knows my secret?* David anxiously wondered. *What will I do if word leaks out?* Sleep eluded him and joy vanished from his life. The anticipation of divine blessing disappeared from the horizon. *Will God ever use me again?* God's hand was heavy on David's heart as he resisted the essential confession and repentance.

"Knock! Knock!" The prophet Nathan arrives for an audience with the king.

It is quite possible that Nathan's visit to confront David for his sin came as no great surprise to the monarch. David's love for God and His holiness had caused tremendous guilt to well up inside long before Nathan made his famous entrance. As he stood before David and prepared to speak, the taut lines on the prophet's face, combined with David's inner guilt, almost make speech superfluous.

David, torn with guilt and fear, waits to hear Nathan out. On the one hand, he is hoping for a prophetic censure so that he can be released from the load he carries. But, knowing the pain that exposure will bring, his flesh hopes for a cloak of secrecy: *Maybe this will never come out. Perhaps Nathan has something else on his mind.*

As David listened, the prophet related the parable of the rich man's confiscation of a poor man's sheep. Relief swept over the king. *Aha!* he thought. *Nathan has come concerning another matter. My sin is still a secret.* Believing his secret to be safe with Bathsheba, himself, and Joab, he responded in proper outrage to Nathan's parable of injustice:"The man who has done this deserves to die!"

Perhaps Nathan allowed an emotionally charged pause before the historic words:"You are the man." Confronted with his sin, great billows of remorse and self-loathing engulf David.

Now drenched in a rich tidal wave of grace, David is astonished that God has any further use for him. Are there words in any language to properly explain such divine largesse? He, the convicted adulterer and murderer, will teach other transgressors? How can this be? Make no mistake about it. Psalm 51, those glorious words that have inspired and encouraged so many sinners, would never have been written if David had not descended into "the dark night of the soul," a prolonged night shift assignment from which he may have doubted he would ever emerge.

Saved . . . to Serve

A sovereign and holy God could have labeled David "useless" and "disposable." Instead, the worthless one became a teacher of transgressors! It was A.W. Tozer who said, "Before God can use a man greatly, He must first hurt him deeply."

All who love Jesus cry out, "Yes! I want to be used. Jesus, please use me!" This is a plea that all would gladly offer, right? But, what about this one?

Dear Lord, I am so desperate to be used for Your glory that I will pay any price You may exact for that privilege. Glorify Yourself through me, regardless of the cost. Please feel free to hurt me as deeply as You desire so that You may use me greatly.

This is a risky prayer. We may think, *What if God takes me seriously? How deeply will He hurt me? Will He overdo it? Can I afford to give God a "blank check" to buffet me?*

The answer, of course, is that a wise and loving God never makes mistakes. He can properly interpret our prayers in a way that is beneficial to us and honoring to His purposes. The good fruit of this final stage of the pit cycle is seen in the fact that David was more useful to God *after* the pit experience than he was *before*. The explanation is quite simple: In spite of our proud self-assessments, it is only God who can truly make an impact on others. As an unbroken horse is of little use for human endeavors, so uneducated vineyard workers can only hinder the production of grapes until broken and retrained by the Owner. How much damage will the employees of the vineyard do to the grapevines until the Owner, under cover of darkness, teaches them proper viticulture? He allows His children to fail and then salvages them for magnificent purposes.

Wired by God for Impact

One of the colossal achievements of the twentieth century was the unraveling of the mysteries of the DNA (deoxyribonucleic acid) code. This code is the carrier for all genetic information for complex organisms. Encrypted in each cell of the human body (except mature red blood cells) is a long, thin DNA fiber. Scientists, by examining merely one of the trillions of cells in our bodies, can deduce a lot about our identity. These DNA fibers control the workings of the cell and eventually dictate our entire body chemistry. Our appearance, interests, proclivities—virtually everything that makes each person different and special—is wrapped up in our DNA composition. This molecular arrangement is the means by which God assigns uniqueness to each human being.

And just as there are no two exactly identical humans on the face of the earth, so there are no two people who function alike in the Kingdom Vineyard. The content of the message we receive and the form of the ministry we undertake as a result of time on the night shift highlights the wisdom of God. He builds into each of His children a sort of "impact DNA" intended to enable each to be used distinctively by Him.

The five components of your impact DNA are:

1. Your wiring from birth

2. Your night shift assignment(s)

3. Your message

4. Your impact venue

5. Your audience

The process goes something like this: First, each person is *wired* from birth to do something distinctive. This internal wiring is the key to what we are best at and what we most enjoy doing. God creates each person to do something exceptionally well, to enjoy that activity, and to bring Him the glory He deserves as we achieve what He created us to do and be.

Second, the vineyard Owner devises a *night shift* assignment that is perfectly suited to the individual. In the language of Stage One, this is The Pit. God's objective is to educate each laborer under cover of darkness. Since only He, the Master Pedagogue, knows best how each one learns, He permits the precise suffering that will enable each individual to achieve maximum effectiveness in the Kingdom Vineyard.

Third, under cover of darkness, He gives each a *message* that is uniquely theirs (Stage Four—The Answer). Our audience will need to hear God's truth and not human wisdom. Night School classes open up the Handbook to us, enabling us to go into the vineyard and to Ethne Market with a message from God on our lips.

Fourth, God creates the perfect *venue* for individuals to carry out their appointed duties in the Kingdom Vineyard. Because the needs are so great and the objectives of the Owner are so lofty, the vineyard is replete with organizational, vocational, and geographical slots in which well-trained Night School graduates may serve the Owner. Whether in the home, the neighborhood, the church, the office, or a ministry, there is a particular niche for each vineyard laborer to fill. No other worker can satisfactorily perform your ministry function in God's work.

Finally, the Owner leads His graduates to an *audience* that no one else can be as effective in reaching. God's method has always been to use His servants to impact other lives for the kingdom. When you are delivered from your night shift assignment, there will be someone prepared by the Owner to receive your message. In other words, there are individuals in need of the vineyard's products, and no other human being can touch those lives in the singular way that God intends to use you.

Ample illustrations of this principle abound in the Bible, church history, and in our own experience. While everyone is called to hear and proclaim the truths of the Word of God, not everyone serves the vineyard Owner in the same fashion. Some have *unique tasks* that no one else is called to do. John the Baptist performed no signs (John 10:41); Jesus performed many. Jesus did not baptize (John 4:2); John baptized multitudes. Joseph publicly prepare a nation for a famine; Elijah hid in seclusion in a widow's home during a famine. James Dobson concentrates on radio work; Billy Graham focuses on public crusades and televised events. Max Lucado writes books; Larnelle Harris sings songs.

Others have a *specialized audience*. Paul felt compelled to preach primarily to the Gentiles; Peter was more at ease with Jews. Jonah was dispatched to Nineveh, while Jeremiah prophesied to Judah. Tony Evans has a calling to the African-American community and racial reconciliation; Hudson Taylor's passion was the Chinese. Woodrow Kroll teaches the Bible to ordinary people who want to grow and mature; Ravi Zacharias responds to the inquiries of the intellectual.

Many have a *specialized message*. Paul stresses salvation by grace through faith apart from works, while James stresses the importance of works as evidence that faith is real. Matthew zeros in on the kingship of Jesus over Israel; Luke concentrates on His humanity as the Son of Man. Chuck Swindoll exhorts individuals to continue on in the Christian life, while R. C. Sproul teaches the great doctrines of the Reformation. Dennis Rainey hammers away at reforming the family, and Chuck Colson exposes the decay of modern culture.

There are no contradictions with any of these. There are different messages given by different people with different styles to different audiences. This is God's way of doing things!

Your wiring, affliction, message, venue for ministry, and audience are all uniquely yours and very useful to God. There is no competition in vineyard labor, for no one can do what you are wired to do, no one has suffered as you have, no one else has the message that is yours, and no other person has access to the venue or audience that the Owner has appointed for you. God has determined that it be so. Yes, graduates of Night School are uniquely useful to make an impact for the Owner.

Surprised by Usefulness

David (and every other Night School graduate) was probably genuinely astounded at the realization that, after his night shift experience, God was using him to influence others. The small place on the night shift tends to change the way we see ourselves. Before the darkness, we are convinced that God's plans will collapse without our direct involvement. But that self-confidence is soon shredded by affliction. The delivered one who makes an impact to the glory of the Lord is constantly astonished. A "clay vessel" bearing precious treasure—what amazing grace!

In high school, I longed to be able to speak publicly, always marveling at others who could communicate in front of a group. But any attempt I made was disastrous. My voice would quaver, my knees would knock, and my thoughts would trail off into confusion. By the time I entered college, I had abandoned all thoughts of public speaking and pursued academic goals that required no speaking skills.

Now, three decades after graduating from college, I am surprised at how much public speaking I do. It is always amazing to discover that I have said something that was comprehensible or that blessed the listener. Once thoroughly convinced by my failure that I had no innate ability to speak before groups, my current usefulness in speaking only assures me that it must be God's grace operating through me. My "failure" was essential for God to receive glory through my "success."

Impact in Little Things

I must be careful lest the implication be given that the *impact* resulting from the night shift is to be quantified by attendance figures, building programs, book sales, dollar signs, or radio and TV programs. The pit survivors whose biographies fill the Scriptures and these pages do not allow us that luxury. Vineyard influence will often be microscopic and shrouded in obscurity. The size of the impact that is made by those who are broken by God through affliction will be as varied and unique as the night shift experiences endured.

Though God may greatly use well-known teachers and ministers, few will have an influence that is geographically wide, financially large, or numerically enormous. Most will prove to be as anonymous as the most invisible of characters on the pages of Scripture. Like the most successful Man who ever lived, we may die with meager visible fruit to show for our efforts.

How tempting it is to magnify the achievements of the more famous celebrities of the Christian faith to the neglect of equally noteworthy but nameless role models. We esteem those who loom like giants on the screen of church history, perhaps unaware of the fact that ordinary people, with an extraordinary God, have always done the lion's share of vineyard work. We dare not succumb to the trap of diminishing the influence of the countless hordes of believers who have privately agonized and ministered on the night shift, far from the public eye.

These who impact others because of their night shift experiences are the little people, people like us, individuals of average means and talent. Most churches are relatively small, believers are generally normal people, pastors are rarely superstars, and the average Christian ministry is . . . well . . . average. The visibility of the faithful is typically minimal. In some cases, like John the Baptist, a faithful servant of the Lord may even seem like a total failure. Contentment with negligible visibility, faithfulness in the quiet corner assigned by God, diligence in the face of opposition—these are the hallmarks of those who have learned their night shift lessons well.

We often hear well-known leaders with large ministries affirm their weakness, deferring all of the credit toward heaven. The glory they give to God is confirmation that such humble leaders have taken their turn on the night shift. Without severe testing and the resultant brokenness, we naturally retain some credit for ourselves.

Only the broken are focused on authenticity. The night shift rids us of our pathetic, small-minded longing for glory. The luster of earthly achievement fades after one has done time on the night shift. Affliction enlarges our vision so that we can see God and ourselves clearly. Once that happens, it's not difficult to figure out who should be the center of attention: God and God alone!

The truly successful servant may never preach a sermon, produce a recording, give an autograph, deliver a lecture, write a book, or speak on Christian radio. But each has immeasurable impact in a multitude of different ways. God opens the doors and the obedient enter the sphere of influence and the venue divinely assigned to them. The humble and contrite understand that the anonymous will also hear a resounding, "Well done, good and faithful slave. You were faithful with a few things, I will put you in charge of many things; enter into the joy of your master" (Matt. 25:21).

A prayer for impact:

Sovereign God, You are for me! I do not need to fear anything that man can do to me. So the large place is Your gift to me from which You will ultimately receive glory. I pray for impact and ask that You would use all of the suffering of my life to bring glory to the name of Jesus. Open up doors for me to preach the message that You have given me through the dark hours of the night shift. Send me to the audience that You have prepared to hear me speak this message. My trust is in You alone. Thank You for Your plan to use me. Amen.

For You have tried us, O God;

You have refined us

as silver is refined.

You brought us into the net;

You laid an oppressive burden

upon our loins.

You made men ride over

our heads;

we went through fire

and through water,

yet You brought us out

into a place of abundance.

Psalm 66:10–12

EPILOGUE

Welcome to the Darkness!

I received a flurry of e-mails from an old college friend who was anticipating joining an established Christian ministry. His enthusiasm for the new venture was almost palpable. Having worked odd jobs for quite some time to make ends meet, he now would have an opportunity to leave the night shift and enter at last the more cheerful environment of day.

A meeting was arranged with the board of directors to finalize his transition into the leadership of this new work. The day after that meeting, I received the following e-mail (somewhat abridged to disguise the identity of my friend and the ministry):

> Greetings to all my family and friends: Please continue to pray. The first board meeting did not go well. It seems that the current leader does not want to give up guiding the ministry, and he is asking me to be terminated. I literally could be without a job in a week. Needless to say, I'm very disappointed in this total turnaround. Thank you for your prayers; I will need them more than ever. . . .

Can't you hear the mournful wail of the night shift in this e-mail? An open door just slammed shut on a faithful servant of the Lord. No explanation given. My friend has had another shift change. As he empties his locker and prepares to switch to day work, he finds his name reentered on the night shift roster. A lengthy stint awaits him before he will emerge from the darkness with a broken spirit, a fresh vision, and a new message.

As I read this e-mail, my mind flashes back almost ten years to April 1, 1991. I, too, had visions of a new and exciting ministry, but I found my name on the night shift roster.

Consider the possibility that you may report for work one day at the gates of the Kingdom Vineyard. As is your custom, you amble over to the employees' bulletin board for the latest news and are shocked to find your name missing from the morning crew. Frantically you scan the bulletin board. *Perhaps it's just an oversight*, you think. Finally, preparing to head over to the Owner's office to investigate, you happen upon the new listing of the night crew. There, horror of horrors, is your name! You have been assigned to work in the darkness, an experience my friend Maria knows all about. . . .

An Awesome Night Shift Assignment

In pursuit of His vineyard objectives, the Owner occasionally requires some employees to work on projects of extended duration—a night shift assignment that staggers the imagination. In such cases, freedom may not result in deliverance, but *a release into God's mysterious mercy, enabling one to work in the dark, with His sustaining grace as the only refuge.* For these special laborers, deliverance is not *from* the night shift but *into* the grace of God.

Maria is a former coworker of mine who has been dedicated to the Kingdom Vineyard for years. She also happens to be one of the most committed night shift laborers I have ever encountered. Such was not always the case.

After serving the vineyard Owner faithfully on the day shift for many years, Maria was thrilled to meet Chuck, a vibrant young believer. Chuck and Maria married and settled down to establish a home. Chuck had an excellent engineering career, and the newlyweds would often talk about their bright future, the children they longed to rear, and their desire to serve the Lord together.

And then one day Chuck and Maria received a new roster assignment that sentenced them to the night crew for the rest of their lives. On a beautiful fall Saturday, Chuck was seriously injured in a hang gliding accident. The initial fear that he would not survive the crash soon gave way to the reality that he would never recover from his injuries. Severe head wounds dictated that he would always be an invalid and that Maria would need to care for her husband as one would look after an infant.

Gone were Maria's bright hopes for the future. Though Chuck was alive, she had lost her expectations for a normal marriage, children, sharing her life with the man of her dreams. Instead, Maria could only expect endless rounds of visits to health-care facilities where nurses would tend to Chuck and where she would watch this wonderful man fail at the most basic elements of living. Her dreams were crushed, and Maria began to struggle with doubt and despair. *How could God allow this?* she wondered. *Where was He when this happened?*

As a reader, you are undoubtedly wondering how Maria's story fits into the finale of this book. Having waded through an analysis of the miserable pit, you are expecting a happy ending, a story of deliverance from the night shift. Instead, you are reading a story of tragedy and apparent hopelessness. Permit me to make my case for concluding with the story of Chuck and Maria.

Teachings on deliverance from affliction can mistakenly lead Christians to conclude that all who trust the Lord will eventually be delivered from the darkness. We may wrongly assume that usefulness in ministry is predicated on rotating off the night shift. Chuck and Maria's story proves otherwise.

Maria's long-term assignment to work under cover of darkness raises important questions that must be answered. Is it actually possible that the vineyard Owner makes *lasting* night shift assignments for certain employees? And, if so, does this mean that these workers will *never* receive an answer from the Lord

(Stage 4)? Will they never experience the joy of deliverance (Stage 5), never sing a new song (Stage 6), never be used to impact others widely (Stage 7)?

Grace under Fire

The chronicle of Chuck and Maria points us to the vineyard's Night School course where the grace of God is the only topic of discussion. Titled "Thorn in the Flesh 401," these lessons are for those to whom the Owner has given a breathtaking assignment of affliction. The text for this course is "Paul's Second Epistle to the Corinthians." Mastery of chapters 11 and 12 is mandatory for graduation, for it is here that sufferers encounter Paul as he pleads for release from his mysterious hardship:

> Because of the surpassing greatness of the revelations, for this reason, to keep me from exalting myself, there was given me a thorn in the flesh, a messenger of Satan to torment me—to keep me from exalting myself! Concerning this I implored the Lord three times that it might leave me. And He has said to me, "My grace is sufficient for you, for power is perfected in weakness." Most gladly, therefore, I will rather boast about my weaknesses, so that the power of Christ may dwell in me. Therefore I am well content with weaknesses, with insults, with distresses, with persecutions, with difficulties, for Christ's sake; for when I am weak, then I am strong (2 Cor. 12:7–10).

When requests for a roster change are submitted and denied, the most precious of all night shift principles is instilled in the laborer: *the grace of God.*

There is a deliverance from the night shift that actually keeps us in the darkness, for it is a deliverance into a deeper understanding of the richness of God's grace. The grace of God transcends suffering and is often best experienced in the midst of interminable misery.

Maria puts it like this:

> This suffering is double-edged. Chuck daily suffers chronic pain and mental torment, trying to understand

why he is not getting better while I watch with a broken heart and with an overwhelming sense of helplessness. But then God faithfully enters the picture and assures us of His love and daily supplies our strength for the day, the hour, the moment. He remains faithful!

Impact! Maria's potential influence on the lives of others is virtually incalculable. This poignant drama—a young wife caring for her invalid husband—is being played out in daily acts of compassion before humans and even observant angels (1 Cor. 11:10; Heb. 13:2). A hush falls over the heavenly host as they gaze in awe at these two laborers, fulfilling their appointed rounds under cover of darkness.

Maria follows in the train of a myriad of "superstar" sufferers who, through the ages, have persisted in working in God's vineyard under unimaginable conditions. These night shift workers operate in a context of astonishing hardship as they care for the elderly, the disabled, the infirm, the dying, the weak, and the despised. They recover from rape; they cope with chemical imbalances in the body; they battle chronic disease, unremitting pain, deprivation, persecution, even martyrdom—all possible aspects of night shift duty.

For the Marias of the vineyard, no tasks are too menial, no unclean or despised person unworthy of their ministry. They work under gloomy vineyard conditions when all human instincts cry, "Quit!" For them, attendance is taken each evening in Night School, and they always show up for class. They are the learners of God's grace, a favor so magnificent that it surpasses the difficulty that requires it. They reflect this marvelous grace to all, human and angelic being alike, who are privileged enough to observe their ministrations.

As Maria's suffering is great, so are the possibilities for her to experience and display the grace of God. She may be all too aware of her failings and inadequacies and underestimate the impact of her ministry. However, there will be nurses, doctors, relatives, friends, and yes, even angels, who will grasp new dimensions of "the gospel of the grace of God" (Acts 20:24) because of her quiet service to the Owner of the vineyard. The prolific output of the vineyard can ultimately be traced back to laborers like Maria, "of whom the world was not worthy" (Heb. 11:38).

Only in Retirement, when all night shift employees have gathered around the throne to hear "tales from the darkness" as told by the greatest night shift Sufferer, only then will all vineyard employees completely understand the full impact and magnificence of the grace of God and the inestimable privilege of extended suffering.

"Man of Sorrows"

Through the centuries, authors, philosophers, and all who have been afflicted have agonized over "the problem of pain." Now, in Retirement, it will be these individuals who will lean forward in eager anticipation to hear the Lamb who once was slain begin yet one more enthralling account of night shift suffering: "Today I want to explain to you what I was doing with Chuck and Maria. . . ."

As He speaks, we see the scars on His perfect hands and realize that we are being initiated into the greatest mystery of the universe. We discover that *He* has always understood our pain. We grasp the concept that *His* sufferings have exceeded all of the hardship of humanity since the Garden of Eden. The voice of authority rings throughout heaven as He unfolds this most complex of all mysteries. We hear reasons, purposes, and elucidations that simply defy human comprehension in space and time. Words too profound for planet Earth will ring with clarity when set before listeners in eternity. And all who hear His explanations will exclaim, "Ah! So that's how pain works! Why couldn't I have understood it when I was in the midst of it? It's a most extraordinary but simple educational technique! God, You are so amazing!" And the courts of heaven will ring with the adulation of redeemed sufferers who now are able to give perfect worship to the "man of sorrows" (Isa. 53:3).

Grace has been the subject of countless authors and hymnists throughout the ages. Of all the words about God's grace that have flowed from the pens of mere mortals, perhaps none have captured this truth for night shift employees better than those of Annie Johnson Flint. Inspired by Paul's words in 2 Corinthians 12:9, she wrote,

> He giveth more grace when the burdens grow greater;
> He sendeth more strength when the labors increase,
> To added affliction He addeth His mercy;
> To multiplied trials, His multiplied peace.
>
> When we have exhausted our store of endurance,
> When our strength has failed ere the day is half done,
> When we reach the end of our hoarded resources,
> Our Father's full giving is only begun.
>
> His love has no limits;
> His grace has no measure;
> His power has no boundary known unto men.
> For out of His infinite riches in Jesus,
> He giveth, and giveth, and giveth again!

No more significant vineyard labor can be found than the ministry of portraying the grace of God in the midst of suffering. Night shift employees who have embraced their assignment, as Paul did in 2 Corinthians 12, are released to have an impact that defies comprehension. Those who have tasted deeply of God's grace are, in Paul's words, "well content with weaknesses." These "grace graduates" are simultaneously in the place of impact and on the night shift. Only the Owner of the vineyard could devise such a plan for displaying His breathtaking grace!

Survival Tips

In closing, I bring three practical tips for your consideration. The disciple who longs to maximize pit time should do three things:

1. Journal. Record your observations, experiences, and thoughts during the night shift cycle. You will come to view this time as precious and vital. But our memories are short and we forget what God has done. I am constantly astounded when I pull out my old journals and discover how much I have forgotten. To fail to remember what God has done is ultimately dishonoring to our Lord, who offers our afflictions as gifts.

When we forget what God has done, we rob Him of the credit He should receive. Where would the Christian church be without the legacy of Hudson Taylor, George Mueller, Jim and Elisabeth Elliot, David Brainerd, and countless others who recorded their thoughts and experiences as a heritage to those who follow them? When we tell our story to others, over and over, "many will see it and fear and will trust in the LORD" (Ps. 40:3). Write it down and you will have a permanent legacy of God's grace to you in the pit. You will remember and share these lessons with others to the glory of God.

2. Give thanks. How simple it is to make this recommendation. How difficult to follow it. Yet thanksgiving is the goal of all conversation with God. As a loving Father, He must grant His permission for all things that come our way. While we may begin with griping, the pit will lead us to gratitude. Therefore, we will learn to thank Him for everything (1 Thess. 5:18).

Thanking God transforms the way we see our night shift assignments. When we thank God for that cranky spouse, unreasonable boss, or flooded basement, we find the object of our frustration transformed. It is so difficult to be angry at something—or someone—for whom we have just given thanks!

Thank Him for the pile of unpaid bills. Thank Him for the cancer that ravages the body. Thank Him for rebellious children, the malfunctioning automobile, the neighbor's dog, the leaky roof, and the clogged drain. By doing this, one's life is consecrated as a temple of perpetual worship. Nothing is excluded from thanksgiving, for He is sovereign over everything that comes our way. And no longer can Satan get the credit for our woes. Instead of shaking our fist at our enemy, we transform afflictions into blessings by acknowledging them as gifts from God.

3. Study Scripture. The best advice I can give is this: When in the dark, master something from Scripture. Like John the Baptist, find a text, a theme, a verse, an idea, a biographical character, anything that applies to your current circumstances, and make it yours. Work it and rework it until you "own" it. This becomes your message for a waiting audience.

How grateful I am for over two years invested in Psalm 40. It is a gift God has given me as a "reward" for time spent in the darkness. The message in this book is my gift from God. It now becomes a present from me (and ultimately from the true Author) to those I meet. It forms the substance of the most important themes in my life and ministry. I look to share this message wherever I go.

Every topic on which I speak carries the weight of my message on the night shift cycle from Psalm 40, for it was learned in the dark. Every child of God should emerge from a prolonged experience in the darkness with something from God's Word that is a personal, lifelong possession. The Word of God—don't leave the shadows without it!

Welcome to the Land of God's Faithfulness!

The panorama of God's awesome plan opens before us. Like a weary traveler who has been wandering through a desert, parched and desperate for refreshment and a change of scenery, we cross over a ridge and there it is! A green, lush valley awaits us below. This is the nature of God's instruction. All who sojourn on this fragile planet in space and time are here for but a nanosecond in contrast to the glorious eternity that awaits us. And here we are learning the truth: God is always sovereign, nothing is wasted, and we work on the night shift at His bidding to do His pleasure for eternal and glorious reasons.

As a postscript to this story, my 1991 night shift assignment was terminated in the fall of 1993 when I was called to the senior pastor position of Stillmeadow Evangelical Free Church in southwest Baltimore. Just when I embraced the idea that I would never return to full-time vocational ministry, this opportunity appeared on the horizon of my life in a most mysterious and serendipitous fashion. In May 1993, I had felt strangely prompted to attend a local evangelistic outreach. Through my presence at this event, I discovered that Stillmeadow's pulpit was vacant.

When I went home that evening, I was carrying the phone number of the chairman of the pastoral search committee.

So it was that in September 1993 I began a six-year period of ministry as the pastor of this church. While pastoring Stillmeadow, I began to teach Bible courses as an adjunct faculty member at Washington Bible College. I was approached by the president of that college regarding the possibility of joining the faculty in a full-time capacity. A transitional period was determined and, by July 1997, I was a full-time professor at Washington Bible College while simultaneously pastoring at Stillmeadow. A year later I added the role of campus pastor to my professorial duties. Though no longer in the pastorate, I am delighted to continue as a member of Stillmeadow Evangelical Free Church with my family and I am blessed to enjoy a warm relationship with the new senior pastor.

This update of my ministry is a brief vignette of grace. I hope it will encourage those who are longing for their borders to be extended. I am always astonished to reflect over my unfolding story of open doors and increased usefulness for the Kingdom. God has granted me untold opportunities to speak, teach, write, lead, and serve the Body of Christ.

I am exhilarated by deliverance and am thoroughly enjoying this season of fruitful ministry. But I am also a realist, and so I view suffering in my life through a practical, biblical lens. Since the night shift is cyclical, fresh night shift assignments undoubtedly await me in the future. Though the prospect of suffering always looms before the child of God, we can know that a loving Heavenly Father can be trusted to determine such assignments by an exercise of infinite wisdom and profound love. I have a new capacity to rest in that love because I have served on the night shift.

This is the intent of this book. No false hope is offered here. We have only the precision of the Word of God to enlighten our eyes to a magnificent truth: *God means it for good!* To celebrate that truth, would you pray a final pit prayer with me? This prayer comes from my lips because my pit experiences have been uniquely mine. Why not change the details of this prayer to conform to the wonderful thing God has been doing in your life under cover of darkness?

A final pit prayer:

Dear Father, for the pit experiences of my life, I give You thanks. Thank You for assigning me to the Land of Forgetfulness without forgetting me. Thank You for the godly men who made up my ordination council and rejected that young, untried, would-be minister. Thank You for the early loss of my mother. Thank You for the terrible mess on my oil hose. Thank You for continuing to do a transforming work in my life that will last through all eternity. I give You thanks in all things, for Your will is perfect. I even thank You for the things that I interpret as evil, knowing that You mean all things for good for those who love You. Amen.

No words can express how much the world owes to sorrow.
Most of the Psalms were born in a wilderness.
Most of the Epistles were written in a prison.
The greatest thoughts of the greatest thinkers
have all passed through the fire.
Take comfort, afflicted Christian!
When God is about to make preeminent use of a man,
He puts him in the fire.

George MacDonald

For consider Him who has endured
such hostility by sinners against Himself,
so that you may not grow weary
and lose heart.

Hebrews 12:3

For additional information about Dave Shive's ministry or writings, or to share your thoughts about *Night Shift,* visit his Web site at http://www.psalm40.net.

To purchase additional copies of *Night Shift* or other related resources from Back to the Bible, visit http://www.resources.backtothebible.org.